Praise for

Gracefully Navigating Anxiety

"Heather's raw and vulnerable account of displaying her own anxiety is incredibly relatable. She has quite obviously leaned into her faith in Jesus and the truth of God's character and nature as a source of strength and healing. She provides practical tools for helping those who struggle similarly to this journey through healing and freedom. In post-Fall life, we can expect there to be struggles — and many deal with debilitating anxiety and depression. With Heather's telling, it is comforting to know we are far from alone, and there is help, hope, and healing available to those who will work at it."

— Mitzi Brown, MA, NCC

"I recommend this book to any woman dealing with anxiety."

— James Fry, Counselor, MA, LMHC

"Heather has leaned into Jesus as He has walked her through the valley of the shadow. He has made her lie down in green pastures and restored her soul as she has wrestled with debilitating anxiety. "Gracefully Navigating Anxiety" offers grace and an unlocked door for those who are ready to turn the doorknob and walk worthy of their calling as a son and daughter of Christ."

— Erin {Squeeze} Willis, Director of *Discipleship Bayside College*

"Anxiety can feel like a daily battle that tries to rob you of your life. We need friends who have walked that truth before us so that we may see there is light ahead. This book will give you resources and a friend for the fight."

— Michelle Rabon, author of *Holy Mess,* editor of *Gracefully Navigating Anxiety*

"An appropriate message for today. Gracefully Navigating Anxiety honors both the person dealing with anxiety and God's Word concerning it. The exercises and tables enable the reader to bring internal thoughts to the surface, acknowledge ways to counter toxic mindsets, and establish a personalized game plan so that anxiety does not rule their lives."

— Christa Eans, *Daytona Dream Center*

"Reading this book is like sitting on a couch and having a conversation with a good friend. Heather brings a raw authenticity by sharing her own journey and what she has learned. You will be invited to have that conversation with your own heart and in prayer. I know I did."

—Kimberly Robertson, Writing Coach, *POV Solutions,* editor of *Gracefully Navigating Anxiety*

GRACEFULLY NAVIGATING ANXIETY

ISBN: 978-1-7374533-0-7
IngramSparks
Cover Design by Heather Frank
Cover Photography provided by www.canva.com/anton_sokolov

While this book is intended as a general information resource drawn from Scripture and psychology, neither the author nor distributors can be held responsible for any loss, claim, or action that may arise from reliance on the information contained in this book. As each person and situation is unique, it is the responsibility of the reader to pursue sound doctrine of Scripture and consult a qualified professional regarding their own personal care.

Photo credits: ©Emily Mathewson (headshot, pages 177, 178), ©Canva.com/Anton_Sokolov (Cover), ©Canva/hooyahphoto (pages 57, 83, 99, 115, 141, 165, 181, 191)

To the man who always points me to the
Lighthouse, Jesus.
Joshua Frank, thank you. I love you.

To our children who remind us of the "why".
Hudson and *Emerson*, your tenderness
and joy shine the brightest in our home.
Never doubt how much we love you.

To my fellow worriers that strive daily to
be conquerors.
This is for you.

"Again Jesus spoke to them, saying, "I am the light of the world. Whoever follows me will not walk in darkness, but will have the light of life."

— *John 8:12*

"When you pass through the waters, I will be with you; and through the rivers, they shall not overwhelm you; when you walk through fire you shall not be burned, and the flame shall not consume you."

— *Isaiah 43:2*

You don't have to navigate the storm of anxiety alone.

GRACEFULLY NAVIGATING ANXIETY

GOSPEL DIRECTION FOR A *PEACE-FILLED MINDSET*

HEATHER FRANK

CONTENTS

Letter from the Author

A weak mind does not equate to weak faith.

Read that again.

And again.

The struggles you face in your mind do not mean you lack faith for restoration. It does not mean you are beyond the hope of repair. And you are not any less valued than the person next to you.

I have to repeat this truth to myself more often than I'd like to admit. It is in the moments when I'm drowning in fear and isolation that I whisper to my troubled soul, "Everything is okay. I am okay." I have a feeling you've been there too. You've walked into a crowd, be it at church, your child's school event, or your weekly meeting at work, and you automatically feel out of place. You look at the confidence of the person next to you and think, "They have no idea what rejection, fear, or anxiety tastes like." If only we knew at that moment, they may be thinking the exact same thing about you. If only we knew in that moment, they too were silently struggling.

I imagine you and I are sitting in my living room, drinking coffee, confiding in one another. We discover an old friend of mine (anxiety) has shown its ugly face to you.

You too feel as if the walls are closing in a room full of doubt and confusion, believing there is no way out. Guilt may quietly creep in, making you believe you brought this upon yourself due to some "lack of faith" movement. I see the sting of shame in your eyes and the weight of worry held on your shoulders. You're at the breaking point I once was, and with this meeting you're holding out for hope. Questions consume your mind, such as, "How can I move forward? How can I transform my mind from the lies that fill my head?" More importantly, "How can we live faithfully as a Christian who struggles with anxiety?"

In my most difficult moments and waves of panic, I sought out books and studies to help me. Reflecting back to my years of study, my undergrad experience in psychology never quite made the answers personal. What was the bridge to navigate this journey as an "anxious" Christ-follower?

The truth in Scripture shows our faith in Jesus can move any size mountain in front of us. This can happen because God says it can (Matthew 17:20). Sometimes He allows the mountain to move. Sometimes He calls us to journey up the mountain.

My story differs from the one told by many former sufferers of anxiety in the church. Unlike some, I have never witnessed that mountain move, or as we can relate, a “healing” of the mind. No. My story is one of Jesus calling me to journey up the mountain for the sake of learning how to gracefully navigate through anxiety. His presence in my life has not meant that I have become radically healed, rather, I am no longer walking this road alone. Like Paul, I have also cried out and prayed fervently in the middle of my own panic for God to “take this thorn in my flesh” and rescue my mind.

Although I would never discredit a radical healing movement in someone else’s journey, that is not my story leading up to this point. To this day I battle the waves of panic, the lies I conjure in my mind, and still walk in the grace of His loving-kindness.

Guilt and fear holds us back from walking in holy confidence more than we would like to admit. It’s the fear of failure, judgment, inadequacy, and having absolutely nothing to contribute, that can be the most crippling in our lives. Did you know that it is more common than you think?

Psychologists categorize three main lies we believe about ourselves[1]:

1) We are unloveable. We are beyond hope of being loved by anyone, and will always be rejected.

I have a tendency to get angry quickly. I can hear my husband snort and whisper under his breath, "You? Never...". I like having my house in order, because once I see an ounce of clutter, my anxiety starts to heighten. I immediately feel overwhelmed, looking around as if a bomb went off. Moms of littles, can you relate? You clean one room just to enter the next, witnessing the damage your toddlers have just done. Seasoned mothers of teenagers, does it get better? I know, it was a cheeky question. This trait we may share is something I am not proud of, and I am trying my best to let God work that out with me. However, because of this terrible quality I unknowingly nurtured throughout my life, I came to the conclusion that I am unlovable. I believed this trait made it easier for someone to reject me, instead of love me. Lie number one.

2) We are incompetent. We lack the necessary skills to accomplish anything or contribute to society.

Growing up, I was a prime target for bullying. I didn't look and act like most girls my age. I enjoyed participating in sports, and related better with the boys I practiced with. I was hardly placed in advanced classes, but I didn't need academic assistance. Put the two together and my childhood bullies had enough ammo to fire at me. When you hear "you're ugly and dumb" long enough, you start to believe it. Have you felt the sting of bullying, too? Lie number two.

3) We are wholly corrupt and unworthy of redemption. As often as we have heard of the gift of salvation through Christ Jesus, we feel we may not be fully acceptable in His eyes. We believe we are beyond the point of redemption. We ultimately feel completely worthless.

My track record is full of dark blemishes. I have done many things that I am not proud of, and I believed God would wipe me out like in the days of Noah. The people were so full of sin and corruption, God found just one man righteous in His eyes. Can our past be so tainted, that He too would turn His back on us because our sin was too great? Lie number three.

These lies do not hold up to the truth in God's Word.

We need to understand the severity of these thoughts in our lives. Allowing God to bring peace to our mind is how we overcome them and truly flourish. God's desire is not to shame us, so we need to immediately break the stigma from this stronghold. He does not condemn us when we find ourselves battling anxiety, because it stems from a normal human emotion: fear. However, He calls us to cast all anxieties on Him, because He cares for us (*1 Peter 5:7).*

This is my attempt to write such a book. My hope and prayer is that you can resonate where I couldn't with other books and studies: We *can* navigate gracefully through anxiety, tying in the struggle and frustration of the journey, all while living faithfully before God, putting our trust in His Word.

If we were sitting beside each other on my couch, I'd refill your coffee (or tea) and tell you that you don't have to silently struggle anymore. Since we are not physically together, I invite you to walk this road of relief and hope with me as we learn more about the Father, and truly understand just how much we can trust in His guidance.

It is possible to flourish as a follower of Christ while actively and gracefully fighting our mental health battles. Although anxiety is categorized as a mental illness[2], please understand that it is one of the most common types. Now more than ever we have seen statistics sky-rocket due to a global pandemic[3], and we need help. There is nothing to be ashamed of in needing Jesus *and* help in mental health!

You are among millions of people that struggle daily with disorders such as anxiety and depression[4]. There is *peace* to be found, and you are certainly not alone. As a fellow sufferer and your ally, I promise there are ways to navigate this hard road. Psychological therapies, prayer, medicine, journaling, there is not one path greater than the other. You have options, and using one or multiple methods are simply the doors out of the dark room in your mind. When we find ourselves in the thick of anxiety, we can become overwhelmed and get swallowed up by it. Rather than allowing ourselves to remain stuck to the point of ruin, we need to get to the point of knowing how to *navigate* through so we can continue on the safe passage to the shore. *The goal isn't to live a life thinking you've defeated all the storms; rather, it's being able to see a storm brewing, acknowledge it, and* ***navigate through it gracefully***. It's learning that we can make it to the other side, regardless if we come out unscathed or not. When you learn how to navigate through it gracefully, you can steer the ship with courage and understanding and not fear the outcome.

Just because you are battling with anxiety, doesn't mean you're bound to it. God is there every day with you to bring light into your darkness, over and over again, as many times as needed. His Word brings truth to the thoughts in our minds that we have filled with negative lies.

As you navigate this book, I pray you learn and wholly accept this truth for your journey. The goal isn't for you to see yourself in my own testimony, rather, you see the heart of God in your own story.

Your friend in the fight,

Heather

Introduction

My parents raised me to be a believer in Jesus. I grew up in church, attending every Sunday school and Wednesday night youth group event. Starting out with simple, artfully composed stories out of the Bible, my journey of biblical education evolved gradually. As a church kid of the early 90's, I was taught by a red tomato and green cucumber on the goodness of God and how His people came to know and be used by Him. "Veggie Tales" and another show named "Super Book" were the two that crafted my Bible knowledge in my early years.

As I approached my teenage years, the simple stories transitioned to fuller passages with intricate details that made a greater impact on not only my knowledge of the Bible, but *how* I viewed God. My idea of this big, almost-intimidating Creator as a child evolved to something more personal. The God I found in those Bible shows was more than this Holy Entity; He was The Father who loved me more than I could comprehend. He was relational, equal parts gentle and powerful. This growth of knowledge and personal relationship didn't stop the freight train that hit head on in those delicate years—anxiety. Since then, I have struggled week in and week out to walk close with the Father while navigating through anxiety.

As I grew older, the yearning to learn more about Him and His word led to an opportunity to attend a ministry school, diving into classes fully dedicated to studying Scripture. Could this be the turning point in casting my anxiousness away?

As a freshly-turned nineteen-year-old in the ministry program, studying looked more like memorizing Scripture, going through the motions of disciplined prayer, and not being completely committed to intimately learning what was in it. We were inspired to develop our relationship with Christ, but rarely diving deep into the Word on the theological basis. I see these words written, I memorize the passage— but what did they truly mean? What was the context? Why did a loving God wipe out civilization (except Noah and his family)? My anxiety stirred wondering if my strongholds would produce the same effect. My lack of understanding produce deceitful interpretation, which then planted lies from the enemy.

Over time I let these lies manifest in my mind, which then birthed panic. If one member of the body of Christ suffers, wouldn't we all suffer? *(1 Cor 12:12)*

I was silently suffering through every wave of a panic attack. Have you ever been rattled by one? At the onset, you feel as if you're in the ocean during a storm, spotting a large wave coming. You feel weightless in the quenching, deep waters, making it seem you are easily destructible. There is no bottom to where your feet dangle, and no means of saving from the open space above your head. Before you can fully grasp what is happening, the 8-foot wave consumes you, taking you under. The weight from the direct hit of water-to-head feels strikingly similar to a blow to the temple from a boxing match. As soon as you can break free from the depths of the water and into the open air, you catch a moment to breathe. Your body feels weak, worn out, and defeated. The feeling of exhaustion leaves you emotionally depleted from the fight. It's terrifying, frightening, and very real.

When I'm in the middle of a storm in life, I think back to the movie "The Perfect Storm". A group of sword-fishermen (and women) risk their lives for their job every day. Heading out for one last cast of the season, they are blindsided by an unheard weather event known as "three merging weather fronts", causing catastrophic conditions in the sea. Each crew member has a vital role to play to help ensure their survival on the ship. There is the Master, the highest rank of Deck Officer, who is responsible for the navigation and safe passage of the ship[1]. The Master is also responsible for the safety and security of the vessel, and the welfare of the crew onboard. These two major responsibilities are just a small part of what they are in charge of.

Next is the Chief Mate, whose responsibility can closely mirror that of the Master. In emergency situations, the Chief Mate is in charge on deck, reporting to the Master as needed. Both help guide the crew safely through the journey[2]. Depending on the severity of anxiety and stress in your life, think of a Counselor as your personal Master and your local church as the Chief Mate who can guide you safely to shore. You need the two to keep you soundly aboard the ship in the storms so that you will not fall out into the crashing waves.

Please hear me when I say this: The right Master and Chief Mate will point you to the Lighthouse, Jesus who is the Light, to guide and help you find safe passage. There are good counselors and churches out there; healthy, life-giving partners to help you. There are also unhealthy, negative counselors and churches. My prayer is that you successfully find healthy leadership in both, and use the two in your journey.

On page 201 you will find resources on how to help you find a local church and counselor.

As I came to believe the truth that my faith was far from weak, I realized I needed to stop beating myself up over my struggles. There is a *need* to push through in seeking Jesus because we cannot navigate this alone. We will fail every time. We don't ignore the raging storm inside us, instead we become proactive in conquering the wave in front of us. Like you, I too am fighting this flesh of mine daily; prayerfully I cling to His grace and not my anxious mind. *I daily humble myself to the point of surrender for the sake of peace in my mind. Jesus did the same, so we have permission to follow His lead.*

"For we do not have a high priest who is unable to sympathize with our weaknesses, but one who in every respect has been tempted as we are, yet without sin." *-Hebrews 4:15*

When Jesus became man, He was tempted by every emotion we experience so that *He would take on the weight of the world in the ultimate surrender.* Understanding this often overlooked detail brought a wave of humility in my storm; knowing He loved me so much, and took on everything that I am experiencing to save me from this chaos. He was no stranger to the temptation that you and I experience when it comes to anxiety, and that should add a mark to our board of trust when implementing guidance from His instruction. He didn't bow down to it. He defeated it.

Sometimes the only way to win is to surrender.

Just as Jesus surrendered to the will of the Father for the sake of our souls, we too need to surrender to the covering of His grace. If I am going to win the war for my soul, mind, and my family, *I must* surrender to His grace in my daily battles. My hope is that you learn this just as I have.

By nature, we don't want to be open and vulnerable, but it's necessary if we want to surrender our anxieties for the hope of peace. Just as Adam and Eve hid in their shame from their first sin in the Garden (*Genesis 3:7-8*), we too want to hide our weaknesses and sin. If we want to reform our minds and live faithfully as Christ-followers, we need to surrender our desire to stay hidden for the sake of restoration in Christ.

Surrender is the moment when you're done fighting with what you *want* to do and succumb to the will of what you *should* do.

I *want* to live a life untouched and unscathed from the worries of this world. I *want* to work out my weaknesses alone and just be. I *want* to stay enclosed, living in the freedom of His lovingkindness while wrestling with my weaknesses, but only for Him to see. However, *an obedient life isn't an easy life*. To obey and say yes is to expose our weaknesses and allow Jesus to do the work in us, which isn't always an easy surrender. This act brings humility, discipleship, and wisdom. I pray that just as I am about to be vulnerable with you, you will be vulnerable with yourself in the coming exercises shared in this book. There is beauty in the surrender and vulnerability.

Even as I have learned techniques on how to face anxiety head-on with intention and courage, the war is not yet won. *I am fighting for peace and finding it in the pages of God's Word*.

I am by no means a Bible scholar, or licensed therapist, as of the writing of this book, I hold a BA in Psychology. With the help and guidance of professionals in both theology and psychology, I am translating my experience and their expertise over to you.

It wasn't until I made a few new friends in my mid-twenties who had the knowledge of the Bible, as I did, but also had a gift of teaching the Word with their whole hearts, that I truly began to understand the meaning of His Word. It wasn't until years later that I truly bridged the emotional side of my relationship to the faithful writings written and inspired by God. **Knowledge is key, love is transformative.** The two go hand-in-hand. This book is about what it means to do that—marrying the knowledge given from His Word with His love displayed in our lives through His grace.

We can live out His peace and the power of the Holy Spirit as Christians who deal with anxiety.

I also have others in mind for the purpose of this book— spouses, parents, children, and close relatives or friends— who are walking this life with loved ones who are suffering, wanting to help navigate with them in this journey to fully depend on Christ. I hope that they, too, can benefit form reading this book.

I want you to know that it doesn't matter how little or how much you know in this area. What matters is that you grow deeper in your knowledge of who God is through His Word, what He says about the struggles we face, and how we can **gracefully navigate anxiety**. We need to go directly to God ourselves to fully comprehend what He says about us, and not to people who interpret what He says. Allow Him to reveal what He needs to for you without a sole interference of someone else's interpretation, *because* He is an intimate and personal God, Father, Friend, and Headship.

Our progress will not be perfect, and that is okay. What is important is that you are progressing forward on this journey. Some days may feel like one step forward, and two steps backward. Please know that is *normal*. Don't allow the hard days to defeat you; just keep moving forward. We need to come to a point where we are *okay with uncertainty* because not every storm we face will look the same. We have confidence in God on our side, so let's rest in that. Let's begin the road to your recovery, even if this is just a starting point for you.

Before You Start

Understand that this book is simply a *guide*. There is not a "one size fits all" method. Work through each page with an open heart and mind.

Get messy in this workbook. Dive into the pages, highlighting and making notes. Get vulnerable. The place of total transparency with ourselves and Jesus is where the healing process begins. Get a trusted person involved in your journey. A partner offers accountability and wise counsel for protection.

Know that you are not alone and there is help out there for you. Together we are breaking the stigma that surrounds mental health. By doing this work you are letting others know it is okay to be vulnerable with your struggles. Having biblical wisdom is seeing our frailty in a damaged world, all while understanding the hope Christ provides. I pray you come to know that there is **peace** and **hope in Christ Jesus**, *even in the midst of our storms.* What matters most is that when you fall, you pick yourself back up again with grace.

"Shame dies when stories are told in safe places."

— Ann Voskamp

This is a safe place.

Know that: You are ***chosen***. You are ***worthy***. You are ***loved***. You are ***seen***.

SOMETIMES, INSTEAD OF
CALMING THE STORMY
WATERS HE SPEAKS **PEACE**
TO US IN THE
MIDDLE OF THE CHAOS.
HE DOESN'T
DISMISS OUR PAIN.
HE DOESN'T
ABANDON US IN THE
STORM.
NO.
HE STEPS INTO THE MESS
OF THE BATTERED BOAT
AND
NAVIGATES THE STORM
WITH US.

CHAPTER ONE

Beautifully Imperfect

"When you pass through the waters, ***I will be with you***; and through the rivers, **they shall not overwhelm you**; **when you walk through fire you shall not be burned**, and the flame shall **not consume you**." *-Isaiah 43:2*

For the first time in my life, my entire body felt like it was completely mutilated. I endured over forty hours of painful labor with my first child. I hadn't slept, my body and mind were worn out to the point of exhaustion.

I was in the hospital room, weaning off the painkillers and coming back to the reality of my battered body. The nurse had just completed her third visit to uncomfortably mash my jelly-like stomach, beating it as if she was pounding a fresh batch of dough.

I looked over at my sleepy husband on the couch nearby, still snoring away, undisturbed by the discomfort I had just experienced.

Suddenly, our fresh-from-heaven baby didn't sound so heavenly with his newfound vocal cords. Thankfully my husband jumped to his feet and reached for him. Not knowing what to do, he handed our babe over to me so I could try to nurse him. As I stretched out my arms to embrace him, all I could think about was how little I knew about what I was doing. What was supposed to come so naturally was the opposite for me: hard, awkward, and unknown. I was created to do this, and yet, I never felt more inadequate than I did in that very moment.

In the days that followed the hospital stay, fear and exhaustion grew. I thought I knew exhaustion until the *crippling fear* of something happening to my new baby made sleep unattainable. Anxiety consumed me over the thought of our son dying in his sleep, or from lack of nutrition. I would beg for him to sleep, but when he would finally rest, I would remain awake to ensure he was still breathing.

It wasn't long before I switched from nursing to formula feeding. Surrendering to that hurdle was a battle in itself. Guilt seeped into my mind as I felt like a failure as a mother. Why did other women have a "breastfed-baby" victory and I could not? Other than the grace and comfort given to me by my husband in that decision, I didn't feel comfort from the Father. I felt unseen by God in my struggles and insecurities because He remained quiet. The feeling of abandonment from God and the demands of a new baby created a bigger storm I didn't see coming. Adding in the raging hormones, exhaustion, and worry, I came face-to-face with the biggest storm yet: *postpartum anxiety*[1].

My mood swings tested my husband's patience and grace. My crying spells were uncontrollable. I dreaded the nights because that meant neither our new son nor myself would get much sleep. In the thick of the moonlit night, I would be half-awake changing my son's diaper while glaring at my peacefully snoring husband. As soon as the routine of feeding our son, changing his diaper, swaddling his body, and rocking him back to sleep played out, my husband would let out a loud snore thus waking our son again. I cried with him as I couldn't start the process all over again. My tears grew hot with anger and bitterness because my husband was the culprit to our son's sudden alertness. If my husband didn't know how I felt at that moment, he would certainly know by morning.

I was running on fumes, and that only fueled my new PPA (postpartum anxiety). The fear of death completely took over my mind, and I felt even more inadequate to ensure my baby's survival. These two circling thoughts of losing everything I had almost became too much to bear. I began to think I wasn't made for motherhood and the struggles that came along with it.

Unfortunately, my fears of the present grew to fears for the future. Would we truly survive this season? Would my son be okay and actually thrive? Would I ever sleep again? Would my husband extend his grace long enough to come out on the other side with me?

In those moments it was so easy for me to succumb to the overwhelming fears that were stirring in my mind. In a season where I felt I couldn't do anything because everything was hard, and the easiest thing I *could* do was worry. It's so easy to worry about what our future holds when we don't have complete control over our current season.

When you are sitting in the quiet and your anxious thoughts start to take over, it's easy to succumb to that moment. It's easier to let worry overtake you, than it is to face the storm head on. You can feel abandoned and unheard. I know, because I have been there. *This feeling of abandonment is far from the truth.*

As I started to come out of the trenches of being a mother to a newborn, and transitioned to one of a toddler, I saw that there was in fact a light at the end of the tunnel. Looking back, I saw I conquered that hard season. We endured the sleepless nights, and my child was happy and thriving. Grace found me every day and deep lessons were learned because Jesus met me right there in the middle of the chaos. When I took the time to open His Word and meet Him, He met with me. I was not defeated. I became a conqueror through Christ in my postpartum anxiety, and you can become one too.

What is Anxiety?

Anxiety is a way your body naturally reacts to stress[2]. Stress affects everyone. We encounter situations in our day-to-day routines and activities that can be less-than-ideal, thus creating a stressful and anxiety-filled situation. Although not necessarily destructive, when prolonged it can have negative effects on our mental and physical well-being, so it's important to learn how to manage it.

When anxiety arises out of a stressful situation, a feeling of fear or uneasiness extends to the future. Some of these feelings of anxiousness are short-lived; like the feeling of the first day of school, a public presentation, or nearing your pregnancy due date. If your feelings of anxiety are extreme and last longer than a small time-span, you may have an anxiety disorder[3].

Anxiety Disorders develop from a very complex set of risk factors such as genetics, brain chemistry, personality, and life events. Some forms of anxiety are Social, Phobias, Panic Disorders, Post-Traumatic Stress Disorder (PTSD), and Obsessive-Compulsive Disorder[4] (OCD). These types of anxieties disrupt your way of life and cause you to stop doing things you would normally do. If left untreated, the anxiety disorder can worsen. It did for me.

My body was reacting to stress and it caused physical problems in addition to the overwhelming feelings of despair and uncertainty. The moments in my life where I felt like I was dying turned out to be *symptoms* of anxiety. The symptoms tricked my mind into thinking any triggering scenario would end me.

It wasn't until I was thirty that I finally realized everything I am sharing with you. It took intentional time during a pandemic, of all things, and time to truly and faithfully practice mental and spiritual healing. In a season where everyone else felt like they had everything to lose, I felt I had nothing left to lose because I was already at my breaking point. I had just finished medical testing with my primary-care physician and a local vascular specialist right before the 2020 pandemic hit. With all results pointing to a great picture of health, we knew anxiety and stress were the culprit to my physiological symptoms. At the onset of the news about the pandemic and quarantine, I knew that if I didn't change, the stress from this new unknown may take me under.

On the following pages I offer up a "Symptoms of Anxiety" scale and the Zung Anxiety Self-Assessment Scale for you to take. The Zung scale is used to measure levels of stress in individuals who have anxiety-related symptoms. It is used for screening purposes only, and not as a tool for diagnosis.

SYMPTOMS OF ANXIETY

CHECK ALL THAT APPLY

PHYSIOLOGICAL

- [ ] POUNDING HEARTBEAT
- [ ] SHORTNESS OF BREATH
- [ ] EXCESSIVE SWEATING
- [ ] CHILLS

- [ ] TREMORS
- [ ] HEADACHES
- [ ] FATIGUE
- [ ] WEAKNESS

- [ ] DIZZINESS
- [ ] INSOMNIA
- [ ] NAUSEA
- [ ] "BUTTERFLIES" IN STOMACH

- [ ] FREQUENT URINATION
- [ ] DIARRHEA

(THE WAY YOUR BODY REACTS)

PSYCHOLOGICAL

- [ ] RACING THOUGHTS
- [ ] IRRATIONAL THOUGHTS
- [ ] IRRITABILITY
- [ ] DIFFICULTY CONCENTRATING

- [ ] RESTLESSNESS
- [ ] DEPRESSIVE SYMPTOMS
- [ ] AVOIDANCE
- [ ] PARANOIA

- [ ] CHRONIC WORRY
- [ ] TROUBLE SLEEPING
- [ ] HATING UNCERTAINTY

(THE WAY YOUR MIND RESPONDS)

PLEASE NOTE: THIS DOES NOT CONSTITUTE A MEDICAL DIAGNOSIS

STRESS FROM ANXIETY

WHAT'S YOUR LEVEL?

FOR SCORING:
A LITTLE OF THE TIME: 1
SOME OF THE TIME: 2
GOOD PART OF THE TIME: 3
MOST OF THE TIME: 4

SCORE	STATEMENT
	I FEEL MORE NERVOUS + ANXIOUS THAN USUAL
	I FEEL AFRAID FOR NO REASON AT ALL
	I GET UPSET EASILY OR FEEL PANICKY
	MY ARMS + LEGS SHAKE
	I AM BOTHERED BY HEADACHES, NECK, + BACK PAIN
	I FEEL WEAK + GET TIRED EASILY
	I CAN FEEL MY HEART BEATING FAST

A __________

FOR SCORING:
A LITTLE OF THE TIME: 1
SOME OF THE TIME: 2
GOOD PART OF THE TIME: 3
MOST OF THE TIME: 4

SCORE	STATEMENT
	I HAVE FAINTING SPELLS OR FEEL LIKE I WILL
	I GET NUMBNESS/TINGLING IN MY FINGERS/TOES
	I AM BOTHERED BY STOMACH ACHES OR INDIGESTION
	I HAVE TO EMPTY MY BLADDER OFTEN
	MY FACE TURNS HOT FREQUENTLY
	I HAVE NIGHTMARES
	I AM BOTHERED BY DIZZY SPELLS

B __________

NOTE THE REVERSAL DIFFERENCE IN SCALING FOR "C"

FOR SCORING:
A LITTLE OF THE TIME: 4
SOME OF THE TIME: 3
GOOD PART OF THE TIME: 2
MOST OF THE TIME: 1

SCORE	STATEMENT
	I FEEL THAT EVERYTHING IS OKAY + NOTHING BAD WILL HAPPEN
	I FEEL CALM + CAN SIT STILL EASILY
	I CAN BREATHE IN + OUT EASILY
	MY HANDS ARE USUALLY DRY + WARM
	I CAN FALL ASLEEP EARLY + GET A GOOD NIGHT'S REST

C __________

SCORE TOTAL:(A+B+C)
☐ NORMAL RANGE: 20-44
☐ MILD-MODERATE: 45-59
☐ MODERATE-SEVERE: 60-74
☐ EXTREME: 75+

PLEASE NOTE: THIS DOES NOT CONSTITUTE A MEDICAL DIAGNOSIS

The phrase, "Something's Gotta Give" rang in my head, and it felt like a clear message from the Holy Spirit.

You see, I've had moments throughout my adolescent and adult seasons where I was taught what freedom in Christ looked like, but up until now, I didn't put it into practice. It's one thing to learn and retain the information given to you. It's completely different to live it out.

I thought my spiritual growth determined my level of anxiety.

I had to start asking myself hard questions, like:

Why is it that I trusted God with my future, yet never fully surrendered my present?

or

When my life feels so out-of-control, why can't I hand it over to the Sovereign One?

Deep down I thought my anxiety was too complicated to overcome. I thought my spiritual growth determined my level of anxiety. Maybe you feel that way, too. Let me tell you, that's a destructive lie we allow ourselves to believe. The lies we believe develop from the way we think.

The way we think matters because it directs what we do and impacts how we feel.

It's Not Supposed to Be Like This

One of the lies we believe is that God isn't there, especially in the midst of our troubles. We mistake what feels like silence for absence. It can *feel* like God isn't there in our battles, because the only thing we hear... is silence.

The way we think matters because it directs what we do and impacts how we feel.

"Fear not, for I am with you; be not dismayed, for I am your God; I will strengthen you, I will help you, I will uphold you with my righteous right hand."
-Isaiah 41:10

We fill this silence with our worst-case scenario fantasies, and over time it manifests, overwhelming us. Being consumed by these lies becomes the master of our lives— in motherhood, friendships, marriage, and career.

It's not supposed to be this way. We have access to the Father who walks with us, and brings peace and comfort that passes all understanding. We have a Father who sees us as the beauty He created, even on our worst days. We are His. He cares greatly about the anxieties we face and how much our hearts can grow weary. What we feel is very real, but so is God. He is the Designer of our very being, and even in our frailty, will walk this path with us.

You are a cherished, beloved woman of God; whether you *feel* seen or not.

Seek His Word

"Seek *first* His kingdom and righteousness, and all of your needs will be added to you" *-Matthew 6:33*

Desiring to learn more about *who* you are and *why* you have the struggles that you do will require the most important step in this journey: learning who *God* is, and how He sees you. To understand the creation, you must go back to the Creator and His story. When we read His Word, not only do we learn more about Him, we see ourselves in the stories of His people. As we are created in His image (the Imago

Dei), we see similar qualities between us and Him. This connection runs deeper than we may ever fully comprehend, and because of that, we simply cannot just depend on ourselves for peace and hope. The self-talk we practice will never measure up to gaining a true self-awareness *in Christ*.

Without Him, half of the healing-puzzle is missing. Why?

We fall short every single time. We have limitations. We are beautifully imperfect, in desperate need of His grace and peace. Within our hurt there are negative thoughts holding us captive. We need to learn the truth in Scripture so that we can counteract what's false, restoring peace to our mind.

This connection runs deeper than we may ever fully comprehend, and because of that, we simply cannot just depend on ourselves for peace and hope.

"We destroy arguments and every lofty opinion raised against the knowledge of God, and take every thought captive to obey Christ." *-2 Corinthians 10:5*

Just as a car needs fuel to run, we need His Word, all so that we can grow and flourish. When we have His words, we can then walk them out. The wisdom given in Scripture can be applied to every aspect of life, especially with our mental health. Rest assured as we dive into the knowledge of what anxiety looks like, and what God says about it, we are laying a biblical foundation we can carry through into our real-world practices.

The heart of God will never conflict with His word, therefore it *should* ease our anxious minds the more we put His instructions into practice. Notice how I said “should” and not “can”? That is because it is tough to learn and apply it while dealing with very real struggles.

You will see that just as much as you and I deal with anxiety and frustration, those in the Bible had it too. Their heart's cry was the same as ours, and through reading their testimonies we are shown there is a God who sees, hears, and restores it all. We see in their strongholds, we have a God who still chose to use them for His glory. *Can you endure knowing the same God who saw and heard their cries, is the same God seeing and hearing you today? Can you navigate this hard road if you remember He delights in your perseverance and strength to combat every false thought? There's hope found in the Father. Don't quit.*

As you begin to dive deeper, it is important to take time to reflect. The questions below helped me to capture my current reality, and allowed me to reflect back throughout my process. I encourage you now to write out your responses below. It's okay to get messy in your responses. He already knows your heart, and loves you just as you are; you just have to get to that place of putting it on paper so you can see it.

What is your view about God, through your anxiety-driven lens?

Now take anxiety out of the equation. Who do you believe God to be?

Do you remember your first panic attack? What happened?

What insecurities do you struggle with handing over to Him?

Lord, I pray as my friend continues this book, You will transform their thinking and aid them in understanding that nothing is too little for You to consider or too big for You to break. You see our anxious hearts, our wavering minds, and You care for us deeply. We thank you so much for that truth. Amen.

WHEN WE GRACEFULLY NAVIGATE ANXIETY. WE ARE CHOOSING TO SURRENDER OUR STRONGHOLDS FOR THE SAKE OF A PEACE-FILLED MIND

CHAPTER TWO

The Hope of the Father

"So when God desired to show more convincingly to the heirs of the promise the unchangeable character of His purpose, **He guaranteed it with an oath**, so that by two unchangeable things, in which **it is impossible for God to lie**, we who have fled for refuge might have strong encouragement to **hold fast to the hope** set before us. We have this as a sure and steadfast anchor of the soul, a hope that enters into the inner place behind the curtain, where Jesus has gone as a forerunner on our behalf, having become a high priest forever after the order of Melchizedek." -*Hebrews 6:17-20*

Unloved.

Unseen.

Uncared for.

These are the words that would sound off in my head as I stared into the mirror. Though you may not physically see these words laid out over my body, they rang true to how I felt internally. They were testaments to my mental health, and wounds that can only be catered to by Jesus.

I wish I would've known then I wasn't a lost cause. After I received my salvation at the age of 11, I grew to learn that my future was secure in Jesus, but I didn't fully comprehend He was more than capable of winning the battle for my mental health, too.

Just as a good, earthly father fights to protect his children, our Heavenly Father is the Ultimate Fighter that wins the war on our behalf. Not only is our future secured in Him because of His great mercy and sovereignty, we can fight our anxious minds daily because He is the path to victory. He is the source of a radically shifted mindset to navigate through anxiety gracefully.

You see, *He is the Perfect Father*, patient in all that He does. Time is no measure in His Sovereignty, and He doesn't need to fast forward to the end result. In this perfect picture of what He creates and how He operates, He values us. He doesn't *need* us, but He *chooses* us. God chooses us because He loves us. My friend and seminary student/writer, Natalia, loves to remind those in turmoil to never forget one sacred truth— "In His abundant grace and mercy, as undeserving as we are, He *chooses us* to be the Imago Dei. God created *us* to represent His very image."

He doesn't need us, but He chooses us. God chooses us because He loves us.

We are chosen because we are loved by Him.

I don't know if you're sitting here today, reading these words, and feel the pain of the past. You may have had a dad who didn't measure up to an earthly standard of what a good father looks like. For that, I am incredibly sorry for your experience.

As God reveals the tender pieces in you, I pray you come to learn that what you have gone through is a result of brokenness and not because of your worth. There is a perfect, Heavenly Father who sets the standard of what love is, and as humans we just cannot measure up to it. However, in our lack He greatly loves us and makes us valuable. If you choose to participate in the refining process, God is there to redeem your past hurts. He can counter your anxiety with His peace, a peace that only He can provide.

Even when our anxieties weigh us down, He is our safe place to bring our burdens in exchange for His peace.

May we choose Him every day... *because we need Him greatly*.

May we choose Him every day... *because we need Him greatly*.
We *need to pursue Him* if we want a holy, unwavering mind. Even when our anxieties weigh us down, He is our safe place to bring our burdens in exchange for His peace.

I am no stranger to anxiety, and although I wouldn't call it a *friend*, it's been an all too familiar foe for the last fifteen years. Like a bird, over time as I stretched my wings, I tried to fly in and out of seasons pretending this unfortunate thorn wasn't present in my life.

By the time my daughter, my second born, turned two, I experienced the crippling weight that stress and anxiety can bring. It reminded me yet again it remained untouched and fiercer than ever. I found myself dizzy throughout the day, elephant-like heaviness on my chest, and frequent drops in my blood pressure. My husband knew to always pick up the phone when I called, because I needed him to calm me down from my panicked state-of-mind. I detailed my long list of symptoms to my doctor, thoroughly convinced I had some sort of brain tumor or heart tremor. Her orders for a heart echo, blood work, and CT scan for my brain only heightened my anxiety further. Once all of the tests came back clear, and my blood work was the epitome of health, we both knew anxiety was the culprit.

I found myself tuning God out, and not following the clear instructions He set out in Scripture on how to handle this stronghold anxiety had over my life. I allowed this perfect storm to brew over the years. Eventually it evolved to such a level that I found myself consumed by it. I needed help. I needed light to shine in the darkness. I remembered the teachings from my earliest years of salvation that

I found myself tuning God out, and not following the clear instructions He set out in Scripture on how to handle this stronghold anxiety had over my life.

The Light was *always* Jesus. Now I needed to believe it.

When the storms roll in, and they will, we need a firm foundation to stand on. We need to shift all of our focus on Him to alter our thinking, so that when stress emerges in life, we can face it *with Him* instead of letting it consume us without Him.

God is *the* Father who will never leave us. The forgiveness and grace He gives is more than we deserve.

In His love I found no shame in my strongholds and struggles. In His wisdom I received assurance to say 'yes' when the unknown shouted 'impossible'.

There was peace.

Freedom.

Beauty for ashes.

Grace upon grace.

I needed a way to handle my anxiety, and His Word became the blueprints for my how-to. Even today, when I come to God's Word, it not only redirects my thinking, but reassures me that He is ever present in my daily struggles. His truth brings light into darkness, and it brought so much light into the darkest parts of my mind.

God sees you, and He cares for you *(1 Peter 5:7)*. He meets you right where you are, being our very present help in times of trouble *(Psalm 46:1)*. I know, because I have walked that path...and I am still a work in progress. I look to Him and trust that He will faithfully guard my heart and my mind just as He has promised in Scripture.

His merciful guidance and instruction laid out for us in His word is everything we need to know to alter our mind.

His merciful guidance and instruction laid out for us in His word is everything we need to know to alter our mind.

Knowing His Character

How can we trust the guidance given in Scripture? We need to understand His character.

I couldn't fully experience peace until I intimately dove into Scripture, learning *who* God is and *why* His instructions give way for a fulfilled life. As I learned about the attributes of God, it not only furthered my knowledge of my Creator, but also alleviated so many of my worries because I knew He was more than capable of being the Sovereign One of my future.

He is the same yesterday, today, and forever.

Learning the character of God should bring us comfort and trust, leading us to apply the guidance from the Father.

Attributes of The Father

Who He is and every aspect of His being aren't man-made ideologies. They are facts given by Him, woven in Scripture for us to read and delight in. Take comfort today in knowing that the God who loved you first, looks like this:

He is infinite and everywhere.

"And He is before all things, and in Him all things hold together" -*Colossians 1:17*

"Great is our Lord, and abundant in power; His understanding is beyond measure." -*Psalm 147:5*

Before creation, He *was* just as much as He *is* present today. We have a God that with great intention created a beautiful universe. He created you with the same intention and care. If you want to learn about the creation, you look to the creator. His understanding surpasses all and in Him, all things are beautifully composed together.

He never changes.

“For I the Lord do not change; therefore you, O children of Jacob, are not consumed." *-Malachi 3:6*

When we read passages in the Bible, we can find comfort because of the mercy and love God shows His people then is the same for us today. We may not be able to put our trust in humanity, because let’s be honest, humanity is just messy. We can, however, put our trust in God who hasn’t nor will ever change. He is the Holy constant in our ever-changing, rugged world. That alone should bring us peace in our uncertainty.

He is self-sufficient, and has no needs.

"For as the Father has life in Himself, so He has granted the Son also to have life in Himself." *-John 5:26*

The God of the universe, having absolutely no needs, knows we have needs. He is self-sustaining, being more than capable of sustaining our every need. He *will* provide our every need, because where we lack, He does not.

He is all powerful.

"Great is our Lord, and abundant in power; His understanding is beyond measure." *-Psalm 147:5*

With His own hand, He created the heavens and the earth. Nothing is too big for His correction and doing, and nothing is too hard for Him to overcome. Take comfort in knowing He is on your side, seeing your struggles, and will equip you to overcome them.

He is everywhere, always.

"Where shall I go from Your Spirit? Or where shall I flee from Your presence? If I ascend to heaven, You are there! If I make my bed in Sheol, You are there! If I take the wings of the morning and dwell in the uttermost parts of the sea, even there Your hand shall lead me, and Your right hand shall hold me." *-Psalm 139:7-10*

When you feel stuck in silence and sheer panic, hold onto the truth that *He will never abandon you*. Satan wants so desperately to separate us from the presence of God, and to feel isolated. That is far from God's will for our lives. In the quiet He is still there. When everything looks chaotic and the frightening panic overwhelms, He is there. He holds us, even in the most troubling of times.

He has endless wisdom.

"Oh, the depth of the riches and wisdom and knowledge of God! How unsearchable are His judgments and how inscrutable His ways!" -*Romans 11:33*

To us, His ways are mysterious and far beyond our comprehension. Just as we cannot fathom what lies at the bottom of the ocean in the deepest parts of it, so is our understanding of His infinite wisdom. Should we rely on our own understanding or trust The One who is full of wisdom with our past, present and future?

He is faithful.

"If we are faithless, He remains faithful—for He cannot deny Himself." -2 Timothy 2:13

"Know therefore that the Lord your God is God, the faithful God who keeps covenant and steadfast love with those who love Him and keep His commandments, to a thousand generations." *-Deuteronomy 7:9*

I don't know your past; but if you've ever been wounded in the area of loyalty, I am here to tell you God never will abandon you. If all you've ever known is painful abandonment, I pray you come to learn and understand *He* will never forsake you. Satan will remind you of your past and will always try to trick your mind, allowing you to believe you are alone to fend for yourself. The isolation creates chaos in us, resulting in a stress-induced anxious state of mind. I pray you come to learn and trust that God is always faithful.

He is kind and full of good will.

"Oh, taste and see that the Lord is good! Blessed is the man who takes refuge in Him!" *-Psalm 34:8*

Pure goodness comes with completely taking refuge in Him. His ways are never meant to bring harm, but only good in your every need. What the world takes and breaks, God takes back and restores. God promises to crown us with beauty for ashes (Isaiah 61:3).

He is just.

"The Rock, His work is perfect, for all His ways are justice. A God of faithfulness and without iniquity, just and upright is He." -*Deuteronomy 32:4*

God knows the very conditions of our hearts, and how we can be fiercely stubborn. He, in His most upright position and wisdom, will allow us to walk hard roads. It's not that we have an unfair, mean God, as His ways are perfect and righteous. He knows the hard roads can sometimes be the only way to lead us back to Him. To guide his children in the way they should go a good father will lovingly give out justice-filled discipline. God is the ultimate Father, guiding and correcting us to live a life flourishing. When we were children, we thought the rules set out for us were restricting and kept us from freedom. It wasn't until we matured with age and wisdom did we realize that a good parent truly had what was best for us in mind. God is just, and His work is perfect in our lives.

He is merciful.

"The steadfast love of the Lord never ceases; his mercies never come to an end; they are new every morning; great is your faithfulness. "The Lord is my portion," says my soul, "therefore I will hope in him."
-Lamentations 3:22-24
"The Lord is good to all, and His mercy is over all that He has made." *-Psalm 145:9*

The Lord is merciful, which is a beautiful complement to Him being just. His compassion for those that love Him is endless, and His mercies are new every day. I am forever grateful that His mercies never cease and are renewed for me daily. Just as I need grace upon grace in my moments, I need His mercies and love equally, if not more.

He is gracious.

"The Lord is gracious and merciful, slow to anger and abounding in steadfast love." *-Psalm 145:8*

He is kind, being slow to anger and quick to give grace, even though we don't deserve it. In the times of our uncertainty, we need to lean on The One who is firm in love, faith, grace, and resolution. If we don't, we will only bow to fear every single time.

He is love.

"Beloved, let us love one another, for love is from God, and whoever loves has been born of God and knows God. Anyone who does not love does not know God, because God is love." *-1 John 4:7-8*

"Love is patient and kind; love does not envy or boast; it is not arrogant or rude. It does not insist on its own way; it is not irritable or resentful; it does not rejoice at wrongdoing, but rejoices with the truth. Love bears all things, believes all things, hopes all things, endures all things. Love never ends." *-1 Corinthians 13:4-8*

It is no wonder that the most perfect attribute that God *is* and has given us gets so damaged in our lives. The enemy takes what is "love", distorts and mangles it, and feeds it to us on a seemingly silver platter. We are fed that love should look one way, taste one way, feel one way; when in reality, it was designed for so much more.

Love is patient and kind, therefore God is patient and kind. Love does not envy or boast, as God does not do one or the other. Love is not arrogant, rude, irritable, or resentful. Love bears and endures all things. God bears our burdens on our behalf, guiding us every step of the way. His perfect example of love was displayed in His son, Jesus. He bore our sin and endured our pain on the cross, and this gave us every reason to not only love others, but give thanks for who we are in Him. You are seen. You are chosen. You are loved. When you find the world shouting definitions of love that doesn't display sacrifice in any light, run the other way. Any other love will only bring destruction and pain.

He is holy.

"..."Holy, holy, holy, is the Lord God Almighty, who was and is and is to come!" *-Revelation 4:8*

"There is none holy like the Lord; there is none besides you; there is no rock like our God." *-1 Samuel 2:2*

He is worthy of complete devotion, because He is good and righteous. In His perfection, without sin, can and chooses to sanctify us in our walk with Him. One day, we will be perfect, free from the strongholds of our mind. This is the hope we have!

He is infinitely glorious.

"And the glory of the Lord went up from the cherub to the threshold of the house, and the house was filled with the cloud, and the court was filled with the brightness of the glory of the Lord." *-Ezekiel 10:4*

The weight of God's glory is measured in good qualities like justice, beauty, honor, and might. The brightness from His glory sheds light into the darkness of our lives because He is full of majesty. He has created all things good in greater quantity and quality, more than we can comprehend.

List three attributes of God that stood out to you the most:

Why did these three stand out to you?

List one attribute that you found the hardest to relate to or understand:

Why is this one the hardest for you to accept?

Write down the verse given with the attribute you struggle most with on a post-it, and put it on your bathroom mirror. For the next week, meditate on that verse once in the morning and right before you go to bed in the evening. What you put in your mind eventually is displayed in your words and actions. Intentionally focusing on truth can help shift your mindset from struggling to accept this attribute, to gladly embracing and trusting this attribute.

Seek His Presence

If we know our God is *good, faithful, peaceful, merciful,* and *full of love* and *justice,* why do we still wrestle with an anxious heart and overwhelmed mind?

Many Christ-followers, if not all, from various backgrounds and genetic makeup, struggle with strongholds. They must deny these daily if they want to remain faithful to the Gospel. Because we live in a dying, sinful world, the struggle is very real. In a perfect, heavenly existence, we would not have to deal with them. God intended our life to be with Him, free of bondage and shame, and our hope is ultimately one day we will be.

In the face of turmoil, we have the hope of *total restoration* one day in His presence. Let's choose to shift our focus on Him. If our focus is on the worries of this world, how can He be our peace?

Right now I want you to trade in simple breathing exercises for *holy meditation* called a Breath Prayer[1]:

Inhale the *repentance*, exhale conviction.

Inhale the *truth*, exhale the hurt.

Inhale the *grace* He has given, exhale *relief*.

We can see God and ourselves in a new light, and we can learn that He is sufficient to meet us in our deepest needs.

Seek His presence as you navigate this journey of anxiety. Stay close to His word, so that you may find the *truth* in the lies.

This is *the how* when it comes to graceful navigation: finding the truth to fight the lies anxiety conjures up in our minds. Trust any time you come to Him in prayer, He is fully present there in your suffering.

Having confidence in who He is and what He says will reshape our thinking from anxiety-driven to graceful freedom. *Are you ready to do the hard, but holy work, of exposing what you've been hiding for far too long?*

"The Lord is near to the brokenhearted and saves the crushed in spirit." *-Psalm 34:18*

"The Lord upholds all who are falling and raises up all who are bowed down. The eyes of all look to you and you give them their food in due season. You open your hand; you satisfy the desire of every living thing. The Lord is righteous in all his ways and kind in all his works. The Lord is near to all who call on him, to all who call on him in truth. He fulfills the desire of those who fear him; he also hears their cry and saves them. The Lord preserves all who love him, but all the wicked he will destroy." *-Psalm 145:14-20*

Having confidence in who He is and what He says will reshape our thinking from anxiety-driven to graceful freedom.

What is the first promise in Psalm 145 that jumps out at you?

What promise in this passage gives you the most hope after reading Chapter 2?

What fear(s) do you have that can be restored through the truth in this passage?

God is good, with no limitations to His power, love, and concern for His people. Are you able to trust His promises given in Scripture after reading Chapter 2?

Lord, as we start the path of understanding anxiety in our lives, I pray You delicately guide us. The battles in our minds are real and fearsome, but we know You are higher than our wavering thoughts. I pray that as we learn the truth of who You are and Your love towards us in our imperfections, we are greatly comforted in Your grace. Thank You for giving us Your direction in Scripture for us to continuously go back to, whispering words of love and not fear into our lives. Amen.

WHEN WE GRACEFULLY NAVIGATE ANXIETY, WE ARE CHOOSING TO TRUST THE FATHER WITH THE PROCESS, EVEN WHEN IT'S HARD

CHAPTER THREE

Exposed

"And He said to his disciples, “Therefore I tell you, **do not be anxious about your life**, what you will eat, nor about your body, what you will put on. For life is more than food, and the body more than clothing. Consider the ravens: they neither sow nor reap, they have neither storehouse nor barn, and yet God feeds them. Of **how much more value are you than the birds**! And which of you by being anxious can add a single hour to his span of life? If then you are not able to do as small a thing as that, **why are you anxious** about the rest?" *-Luke 12:22-26*

I was so afraid my faith would be tested and I would have to walk through the fire of losing my children. I couldn’t fathom how I would respond to such a devastating circumstance, and begged

God for any other test but that. People I know and read about have grown stronger in their faith from walking through the fire. Some of them have experienced the unimaginable, and because of their unwavering faith in Jesus, it sparked a different way of thinking in those around them.

Their testimony held a candle to my anxious thoughts, exposing what needed to be refined for God to continuously work in me. Witnessing them navigate such devastation convicted the deepest parts of my being. How can they meet face-to-face with my deepest fear, and still give all glory and praise to God?

I wrestled hard.

It challenged me to dive deeper to find the faith I lacked. Their transparency revealed it was no little feat, and most days they didn't want to do it. They had nothing left but to pursue the Father, and in return, He graciously poured out His love and comfort over them. I always wanted that intimate relationship with God, but I feared what it would cost to get there as it did them. I want to control the process so that I can avoid the pain. Don't we all?

One of the greatest fears we possess is the fear of dying[1]. We fear death because it's the greatest unknown to man. We cannot truly comprehend what it's like to die, and that can be utterly frightening. What we know of death is only from an outside experience marred by grief felt by a loved one or a stranger.

Death puts life into perspective - it is fragile and temporary. Just ask any military wife how they feel every time their spouse receives a draft order. They are left months with the absence of their presence and fear for the unknown.

The powerful emotion we feel associated with death can develop into a *trigger*[2]. A trigger is a psychological stimulus affecting your emotional state, causing distress and extreme devastation. The trigger doesn't have to be something strenuous, and it could be as simple as a certain scent or item. If a child I loved drowned in a swimming pool, seeing a pool can trigger the pain of their passing. Once the association has been made, these emotions become building blocks for a thought structure that is far from stable, and could lead to destruction. If I allowed this to manifest, I may never again allow my own children to swim without my presence, or walk on eggshells being near a pond, knowing tiny feet are walking nearby.

Triggers are our teachers, if we allow them to be. If we commit to shift our mindset, we can view them as a tool in the aid of learning about our anxiety. If we know what is triggering us and why, then we can respond in new ways that align with God's truth.

Feeling the weight and devastation of loss is not what is unhealthy; it's allowing the weight to consume our entire being that can be devastating.

We in our human nature feel emotion because God the Father designed us to feel. We see this in the book of John. The death of Lazarus caused great sorrow in Jesus' heart, even though He knew He would raise him from the dead *(John 11:33-44).*

When we get stuck in the ruin and let anxiety consume us, it can lead to a bigger problem. We can feel the walls closing in and our own time is now more limited, and it can end at any moment. We have created a trigger that causes our anxiety to take hold once again.

This Is Freedom

Walking in true freedom looks like a holy mindshift completely trusting- "God's got this!"

Our triggers will never fully go away until we are *with Jesus*, so until then, let's stay focused on Him and not the false realities we conjure up in our minds.

Reflecting back to the passage in Luke 12:22-26, consider that if ravens are fed and provided for by God - how can we be anxious when we are image-bearers of God? *(Genesis 1:27)* As the Imago Dei, we are far more valued than the ravens. We have the opportunity to be redeemed, provided for, and set free when our minds are focused on Him.

Considering this truth, I often ask myself:

"If God has appointed these children to my husband and I, and He fulfills our every need, why can I not trust Him with their future?"

We cannot always see His inner-workings in our life, but we can trust the unseen because something *is* happening *(Hebrews 11:1)*. However, we can trust and have faith that *everything is working for good to those of us that love Him* (*Romans 8:28)*. This is where faith can truly move mountains.

I know it's hard to fully surrender everything to Him. I get it. Every season of my life I have danced with anxiety, it was for very different reasons, but the same worries. Whether it's finances, housing, health, or traveling, it still remains a thorn in my flesh to this day. There was a period of time in my life where I would be terrified to even mutter these words:

"*Lord, these are Your children. I trust that You will protect them. I trust that even if a situation does not go in my favor, and I am found in agony, You are still good. I give their lives into Your hands.*"

This emotional trigger of mine exposes a weak area of my life that I am unsatisfied with: the control of what happens to my own children.

This *emotional trigger* of mine exposes a weak area of my life that I am unsatisfied with: the control of what happens to my own children. Yes, hearing of a child dying is horrific and devastating. Feeling a sense of empathy toward the parent, anger that a young life has been taken away, and sadness for the child are all *justifiable* feelings to possess. However, there can be a deeper root to the hurt. When you look at your own triggers, you can trace your way back to the source of pain.

My entire life I felt like I was inadequate in almost anything and everything I tried to accomplish. I believed I could never measure up to my classmates' advanced placements in academics. I failed at placing in the prestigious first-choice colleges, and was never considered for an athletic scholarship. My test scores were two points under the requirement of the average scholarship, and our household income couldn't touch any type of leeway in the matter. I did find wins throughout my life, and yet, I allowed the whispered lies to drown out the triumphs. And so, in becoming a mother, I'm now given the biggest mission of all: stewarding my time as a mother well, whether our time together was short or for the long haul.

In my mind, I took the truth of motherhood that, "this new life is completely dependent on mine", and my anxiety turned that thought into, "this life is completely dependent on mine and I am ill-equipped and not suitable for this job". The fear of getting into a car crash with my children became crippling.

If they choke, will I be able to get the lodged item out so they can breathe?

What if they were near an open body of water and didn't know how to swim yet?

Worst-case scenarios would emerge time and time again, and I felt incompetent, unable to keep my children alive.

I allowed the "what ifs" to create a revolving door of fear, rather than dwell in an "even if" state of mind for a more faithful-led life.

I allowed the "what ifs" to create a revolving door of fear, rather than dwell in an "even if" state of mind for a more faithful-led life.

I needed to get to a point where I could believe,

"Even if my children are injured, I will do my best to help them. Even if I fail and lose my cool on them one day, new mercies are given every day, and I will try again. "

The weight of the situation should not determine when you trade out the What If for the Even If. In every circumstance, we need to get to the point of "even if", because that will be led by faith and not fear.

Becoming aware of your triggers and writing them down is a first step towards emotional healing. Not only does this bring clarity, but it creates a setting of vulnerability. If we want restoration, we must expose our weaknesses for the process to begin.

List a few triggers that you may have recognized for yourself on the following page (you can also extend your notes on pages 238-241):

TRIGGERS

WHAT TRIGGERS MY ANXIETY?

DRIVING BECAUSE I HAVE BEEN IN TOO MANY CAR ACCIDENTS TO COUNT. SEEING LITTLE FEET NEAR AN OPEN BODY OF WATER BECAUSE I HAVE HAD A CLOSE FRIEND DROWN AT A YOUNG AGE...

WAYS YOU CAN OVERCOME YOUR TRIGGERS:

- ◯ AWARENESS | MAKING A LIST BRINGS CLARITY
- ◯ TRACK IT | GET TO THE ROOT OF WHEN IT STARTED
- ◯ REPROGRAM | REPLACE NEGATIVE BELIEF WITH POSITIVE
- ◯ SPEAK LIFE | YOU BECOME WHAT YOU SPEAK
- ◯ SEEK HELP | PROFESSIONAL GUIDANCE IS PROTECTION

Where do you think these triggers originated? My crippling fear of driving came from a few car accidents I experienced in my early driving years, one of which caused me to completely black out. My mind has no memory of how it happened, but my body remembers every detail. The fear of losing my children goes back to witnessing multiple childhood deaths growing up.

If we want restoration, we must expose our weaknesses for the process to begin.

Were you neglected as a child growing up from a parent or caregiver? Did a teacher call you out in school and make you feel belittled in front of your classmates? Did a family member make crude comments about your appearance? Figuring out where the hurt originated reveals why you may feel the heavy weight of the trigger today. There will always be a root to every fear/trauma. Knowing where our triggers come from contributes another piece to the healing puzzle.

What Does God Say About Me?

Examining one trigger at a time and holding it up to God's truth leads you to the path of reprogramming those negative beliefs. It's saying, "That is not true. This is not reality. The truth is, God sees me. He has created me to be loved and a conqueror. I have wisdom because He has given it to me. I am who I am because the Ultimate Creator made me who I am with intentionality."

Examining one trigger at a time and holding it up to God's truth leads you to the path of reprogramming those negative beliefs.

When we start reciting Scripture back to ourselves, in writing or aloud, we are actively working towards reprogramming the way we think.

"...in Christ Jesus our Lord, in whom we have boldness and access with confidence through our faith in him." -*Ephesians 3:11-12*

You are not what your past hurts said you are. Walking in the boldness Christ has given us allows us to gradually and firmly believe we are who He says we are in Scripture. God doesn't breathe words into Scripture *just because;* our Ultimate Counselor has given us instructions on how to navigate life. He tells us to cast all worries onto Him, leaning not onto our own understanding, and that He is greater than our deepest fears. Our own understanding shouts *failure*, but His infinite wisdom whispers *conqueror*.

A life of faithful obedience to His guidance is not an easy one to live out, but His Sovereignty is over us, always! He is the God who redeems and restores us. He uses His people to support us in our healing journey. Allow a trusted friend or professional to aid in your healing journey as well. *Give yourself grace and permission to do so, because it's more than okay to ask for help!*

"Where there is no guidance, a people falls, but in an abundance of counselors there is safety." *-Proverbs 11:14*

Lord, I pray for peace that passes all understanding as we navigate our fears and triggers. I ask for Your wisdom and comfort as we pinpoint what anxiety looks like in our life, along with our personal triggers. We acknowledge You are greater than our weaknesses, and higher than our uphill climb in this mental health battle. I thank You for Your grace, mercy, and love in this journey. Amen.

WHEN WE GRACEFULLY NAVIGATE ANXIETY. WE ARE CHOOSING TO HUMBLY EXPOSE OUR WEAKNESSES IN EXCHANGE FOR LOVING GUIDANCE

CHAPTER FOUR

It's Okay to Ask for Help

"**Whatever you ask in my name**, **this I will do**, that the Father may be glorified in the Son. If you ask me anything in my name, **I will do it**."
-John 14:13-14

I had the hopes and dreams of attending a major theological university, and set my mind solely on that my entire senior year of High School. Yet, at eighteen years old I found myself attending a local community college.

Like any other high school senior, when your mind is set on a certain path, it's hard to look anywhere else. The summer after my senior year of high school, I realized not only did I not get enough money in scholarships and grants, I did not have enough money in savings. This path was my first and only-choice, and it was not cheap. I could not afford my dream college experience, and had to resort to the local community college. I felt like a failure.

A couple of months went by, and I was unhappy. I was unable to release this season to God and, instead, allowed an anger-driven attitude to initiate the perfect storm. I felt anxious and embarrassed when seeing classmates from high school in the hallways. Bitterness became my companion. The stress and shame built up, creating a season that would alter my life to follow.

I was sitting in my Code of Ethics class, and the professor was assigning our first public presentation project. Without warning, I felt my face getting hot, my palms began sweating, and the room started to close in on me. My heart began to race, and dizziness overtook me.

In the middle of the lecture, I grabbed my bag and sprinted out of the classroom. I clutched the wall, bending over trying to breathe. Thoughts raged, "Am I dying? Is my sugar low? Why am I so dizzy? Do I need to call 911?" I had never experienced the immense pressure on my chest and dizziness until that day.

The next week I experienced another episode - same classroom, same time. It stirred a fear inside me. This particular classroom felt as if I had no room to escape. I let that fear consume me and little by little, the panic I was experiencing manifested in all my classes.

Soon the anxiety was so severe it progressed beyond attending my lectures. I couldn't go to a movie without feeling trapped, and had to leave mid-show. I couldn't go out to eat anymore because it was hard to breathe, and I developed a fear of choking on my food.

At the time I didn't know what I was experiencing. It wasn't until my mid twenties that I learned it was a *panic attack*[1]. As mentioned previously, the cycle of a panic attack is more than crippling.

Panic Attacks

Many mistake it for a heart attack their *first time* encountering one; I was one of them.

As the years went on, my association with interstate driving and terror progressed to driving altogether. What was once a simple task to drive to school, appointments, and work turned into terrifying tasks. I would call my mom to talk me out of my panic attack so I could compose myself to turn around and just drive home. I made excuses why I couldn't drive to events because of how far away they were. If friends were planning a getaway or a girl's night out, I would have to carpool so that I could be involved. It took years for me to even open up about why I would not, or could not drive.

Anxiety seeped into every area of my life, and I needed help. Once I became open about my struggles, my family and friends were more than understanding.

I'll never forget the day my cousin, Ellen, drove me to the doctor's office. I couldn't drive myself to an appointment because of the panic, and my husband's work schedule was more than demanding. In his plea he suggested it was time to involve the family. In my desperation I sent out a white-flag surrendering-like signal that I needed help.

While my other cousin, Michelle, stayed home with my two children, Ellen drove us to my appointment. Despite the weight of heaviness on my chest, I tearfully felt relief I was heading in a direction of hope. Walking into the doctor's office that day paved the way to the road of relief.

My health professional and I discussed what was making my heart and mind anxious, and what my options looked like. Resting under the care of a fellow Christ-follower who just so happened to also be my nurse practitioner gave permission for me to trust her insight and wisdom.

On the drive home, with a hopeful prescription in hand, my cousin opened up to me about her own mental health struggle. Vulnerability, compassion, and relief created the aroma in the car that day. To this day I am grateful for that moment.

It opened a door for me to know that I was not alone, and that others experienced anxiety, just in different areas of their lives.

I was not alone, and you my friend, are not alone either. It's okay to ask for help.

I was not alone, and you, my friend, are not alone either. It's okay to ask for help.

When the Darkness Lingers

Cognitive Behavioral Therapy, medication, Exposure Therapy, and Relaxation Techniques are all ways to treat anxiety[2]. One is not superior to the other. All have benefits when used properly and with professional guidance, and all can be a part of your healing process. I needed help to get my mental health back. The medication my doctor prescribed was an antidepressant to treat my anxiety. Antidepressants are Selective Serotonin Reuptake Inhibitors (*SSRIs*) that affect your brain chemistry by slowing the reabsorption of the neurotransmitter *serotonin*[3]. This neurotransmitter helps regulate mood and *anxiety*, thus relieving anxiety symptoms. Although SSRI's are the most often prescribed, SNRI's, and DNRI's are also main line prescription therapies.

Jot down some of your preconceived notions regarding medication for anxiety:

Please hear me when I say, sometimes medication *is* necessary. We need help physiologically to get us back to a place where we can function properly. We are born into this sinful world and because of that, there are plenty of weaknesses in our being (Genesis 3).

When I felt swallowed in the sea of panic, I intentionally sought out Christ more diligently, all while using low-dose medication. In time I began to perform normal routines, and stress began to melt away. I then reassessed with my health professional. With her guidance, I was able to wean off my medication and live life managing my anxiety without it.

I want you to know that it is *okay* to have this form of relief in mental health. God has given us the knowledge and use of medicine to accommodate the needs of our physical bodies. There would be no need for medicine if we were perfect.

Just as there is no stigma in attending to our physiological needs, there needs to be the same standard in treating our psychological needs. As a supportive friend, I would tell you to drink water daily to stay hydrated, take your vitamins, and move your body for overall physical wellness. In the same breath, I will tell you to take care of yourself mentally with the help of professionals. We may do so well with keeping a log of our water intake, but are we keeping track of our mental health?

Journal

Keeping a log of panic attacks and triggers is helpful in your journey. It allows you to look back, see progress, and refer to it in a counseling session. Starting on page 232, you'll find space to log in your anxiety/panic track record. You'll see a right-sided margin dedicated to additional note-taking. Use it as an option to extend on what triggered your anxiety and panic, and any other additional thoughts you may have for that month. The more detail, the better awareness you will have. Not only can this help equip you to prevent future attacks, it becomes a written testimony of how far you've come.

Breathing

Breathing is *so* important while you face a panic attack. Driving can trigger my own panic attacks; it is especially important for me to breathe so I can avoid a car crash. What was once hard for me to admit, I am here to tell you today I have often pulled over so I could work through my attack. Those moments are now far and few in-between as I still navigate this journey. What changed? Breathing through the panic, reciting Scripture that I intentionally memorized to meditate on through the exercise.

One of the most popular *breathing techniques* is called the *4-7-8 method*[4]. After reading the instructions, go back and practice.

Close your mouth, and inhale slowly counting to 4 in your head. Hold your breath for 7 seconds, and then slowly exhale counting to eight. This is one breath. Repeat once more.

How do you feel?

This breathing technique allows your focus to shift from hyperventilation, to a peaceful rhythm, thus calming your mind. It allows you to focus on the present, rather than imagining the worst-case scenario.

It brings a moment to calm the sensory overload, giving you an opportunity to shift your focus on the Truth you have learned in God's word (the moment can look like looking at a post-it note you created with Scripture, or opening up the Bible app on your phone). When He doesn't feel present, we can quiet our mind to reflect back on the Truth that He is always with us. We can use this practical tool to put a stop to the attack, so we can shift our focus back to Him, the Sovereign One who is ultimately in control.

Nutrition

I've always known what we eat matters, but little did I know how much it affects our mental health! We have learned what serotonin is, but do we really know where it's found in our bodies? I'll be honest, I didn't know, nor did I care.

The cells in our body produce a chemical nerve called serotonin, which is mostly found in our *digestive system*[5]. We know that serotonin is a natural mood stabilizer. It helps with sleeping, eating, and digesting. It is made from the essential amino acid Tryptophan[6].

Does Tryptophan ring any bells to you? It's the sleepy component found in turkey. Now we know why we sleep after Thanksgiving dinner.

Tryptophan helps regulate many physiological mechanisms in our body, acting as a mood regulator. Have a deficiency in tryptophan? That can lead to lower serotonin levels, which can then result in anxiety or depression. It's not the sole reason for lower serotonin levels, but it can be a cause. The goal is to have serotonin levels normal because then we feel happier, calmer, more focused, less anxious, and overall more emotionally stable.

Studies I found do disagree if ingesting foods enriched with tryptophan will make a difference with serotonin levels[7]. However, there are professionals who suggest taking a supplement of purified tryptophan to increase brain serotonin.

Your doctor can recommend tests to assess your physical health to achieve overall mental and physical well-being. It might take a complete diet shift, or simply adding a few vitamin supplements.

Anxiety isn't the cause, but merely a "notification" that something isn't right, like a check engine light going off in your car. As you're driving you hear a *ding*, and then you take notice of that pesky orange engine light shining bright. *There's something wrong*, and if you don't address it soon, bigger problems will arise.

Anxiety plays the same role in our lives. There is something going on in your life that is causing a great amount of stress. Whether it's outside influencers of stress, or something you're mentally wrestling with, it's becoming too much. It could be a warning that something else is going on inside your body, such as a Vitamin B12 deficiency[8] for example. God is our Great Physician and He gives wisdom to people, such as our doctors, to use

> *God is our Great Physician and He gives wisdom to people, such as our doctors, to use science to help identify what our bodies may be lacking.*

science to help identify what our bodies may be lacking.

Remember what I said from the beginning that a weak mind does not equate weak faith? Sometimes, there's more beneath the surface, like a chemical imbalance or vitamin deficiency causing your 'check engine light' to go off. Learning the why in our physiological responses can bring relief because there's power in knowledge. When we learn that our troubles may very well be just from anxiety, it can bring peace because there's work to do in our minds. If there are other underlying causes, we then take the next steps to fix the problem. *Will you reach out today in setting up that appointment? Will you take that step in working this process out?*

Lord, we thank You for the wisdom given to doctors and therapists to aid us when our bodies fail us. We thank You for your grace given in every situation we face, and Your perfect guidance freely given on how to navigate our strongholds. May we give ourselves grace when we feel inadequate, and permission to humbly follow your guidance and the instructions of our doctors for the sake of a peace-filled mind. Amen.

WHEN WE GRACEFULLY NAVIGATE ANXIETY, WE ARE CHOOSING TO FAITHFULLY WALK UNDER THE INSTRUCTION OF THE FATHER

CHAPTER FIVE

Working it Out

"But on the first day of the week, at early dawn, they went to the tomb, taking the spices they had prepared. And they found the stone rolled away from the tomb, but when they went in they did not find the body of the Lord Jesus. While **they were perplexed about this**, behold, two men stood by them in dazzling apparel. And as they were frightened and bowed their faces to the ground, the men said to them, "**Why do you seek the living among the dead? He is not here, but has risen**. ***Remember how he told you***, while he was still in Galilee, that the Son of Man must be delivered into the hands of sinful men and be crucified and on the third day rise." And **they remembered His words**." *-Luke 24:1-8*

I experienced breaking, reshaping, and molding while

growing in Christ and pursuing peace. I had to reject the pull of fear in me and press into His holy presence daily. I had to do the hard but holy work of, rather than treating God as a once-a-week dosage, I needed to seek Him as my daily every-meal bread. Food is the sweet picture of the daily nourishment process. If someone doesn't eat, they become weak and sick. We need to consume His word and rely on Him so that we may live and flourish.

During Jesus' earthly ministry, He revealed to the disciples His purpose: He would die to redeem all of humanity. His followers were told by Jesus *Himself* His death was coming, and He would *rise* again.

However, when the moment came, they still felt abandoned. Everything they knew was upside down because their Savior was crucified and laid to rest in the tomb before their eyes. They had forgotten the multiple reminders given by their King, and were left with the echoes of His death. Even though Christ prepared them for His death and resurrection their faith wavered when all felt lost. They didn't fully work out the Truth that was given to them.

Even in the dark silence of disconnection, He is working, comforting, and bringing peace.

The disciples surely felt anxiety, raising to the surface more "what ifs" than the truth they were told. For those of us that deal with anxiety, we too face the same harsh echoes in our minds. We allow the lies to rage on, creating a false, dark reality. We unconsciously give permission for this mind-war to consume us, leaving us alone and damaged. In Genesis 1:1-2, when God spoke light into the dark, He brought order from the empty void and chaos. In Luke 23 and 24, what seemed hopeless to the disciples, was the unfolding of Christ's redeeming light.

Even in the dark silence of disconnection, He is working, comforting, and bringing peace.

Our darkness can be mirrored to the three days following the death of Jesus. When you feel defeated and as if He is not present, meditate on the truth that He *is there*.

He went silent on Friday, but rose again on Sunday.

The Light was brought out of the darkness
claiming victory and redemption.

He too can bring His light into your darkness,
claiming victory over a wavering mind.

Your Sunday is coming.

How are you doing so far? If you have been actively engaging in more alone time with God, have you noticed a difference in your days yet?

If you have, list what you have changed or implemented into your daily routine to better your overall spiritual and mental health:

To produce different results, you need to apply different techniques. This is the ultimate picture of doing the hard work in gracefully navigating anxiety. The process of removing unwanted impurities or elements in your life produces the ideal outcome, which also looks like refinement. Over and over again we must address and reassess where we stand in the journey with simple, but powerful, techniques.

Methods of Coping with Anxiety

Here are suggestions to keep in mind as you learn ***how to cope with your anxiety***:

- **Do your best.** Understand you are human, and perfection is non-existent. There is only one man who is perfect, and His name is Jesus. As we walk our path of sanctification, the most important thing to remember is to *do your best*. ("For we all stumble in many ways. And if anyone does not stumble in what he says, he is a perfect man, able also to bridle his whole body." *-James 3:2*)

- **Accept that you cannot control everything.** A lot of things in our life, if not most, are simply out of our hands. There is freedom in learning that we possess the illusion of control, but not control itself. This should take the weight off of our shoulders, and eliminate yearning for perfection. ("...all the inhabitants of the earth are accounted as nothing, and He does according to His will among the host of heaven and among the inhabitants of the earth;..." *-Daniel 4:35*)

- **Face your anxieties head on, one at a time; casting each one onto God.** Refer to your *Panic Attack Log* (in the back of this book) and recite each trigger out loud to God. Reflecting on the truth God can equip you to deal with your triggers and panic attacks can be helpful in the process of casting them onto Him. ("Casting all your anxieties on Him, because He cares for you." *-1 Peter 5:7*)

- **Relax, and breathe.** Focus on your breathing and prayer to cast your fears onto God. Remember to initiate the *4-7-8 Method* when needed. Play your favorite worship (or meditation) music playlist to focus your breathing in the moment of anxiousness. ("Do not be anxious about anything, but in everything by prayer and supplication with thanksgiving let your requests be made known to God." *-Philippians 4:6*)

- **Break the cycle of worry.** We may have found that we are not the first in our families to experience anxiety, but we can fight hard to be the last. Your efforts and prayers now can have an eternal impact. You are a breaker of chains and an inviter of spiritual freedom. We have the power and opportunity to break the strongholds in our lives. ("Therefore do not be anxious about tomorrow, for tomorrow will be anxious for itself..." *-Matthew 6:34*)

- **Get enough sleep**. It is *holy* to practice rest. God Himself rested on the seventh day of creating the heavens and the earth. His rest translates simply as "stopping"- to halt all work. For us, in our human form we need sleep to restore. Our bodies and minds need a reset, and a proper one at that. Depending on your needs, six to nine hours is sufficient for adults[1]. You may notice the day following an unrestful night's sleep leads to heightened emotions and uneasy physiological symptoms, like headaches and fogginess. Get that rest! ("In peace I will both lie down and sleep; for You alone, O Lord, make me dwell in safety." -*Psalm 4:8*)

- **Reduce/Eliminate Caffeine & Alcohol.** Caffeine is a stimulant, which can activate the "fight or flight" response, possibly triggering a panic attack[2]. Alcohol changes levels of serotonin and other neurotransmitters in the brain, which can worsen anxiety[3]. It's socially acceptable, and even encouraged, to start and end your day *heavily* with one or both substances. It's no wonder those of us that are suffering are lost in a crazy cycle of anxious spinning. Increase your water intake, decrease your caffeine intake. Replace those glasses of wine for a walk around the block with your family. I happily sip my iced coffee in the morning following a good work out, and may enjoy an adult beverage socially here and there. I have come to understand that the more depressants/stimulants I give to my body, the more anxious I feel from the stimulant responses from caffeine, and my panic attacks may be more frequent. If you are on medication for your anxiety, there are warning labels to avoid alcohol. Take in the knowledge of why there are warning labels, and use wisdom in your daily intake.

- **Overcome triggers with controlled exposure.**

Refer to your list of triggers in your *Trigger Tracker*. Learning what your triggers are and how they happen will help you limit exposure. Driving on the interstate is a trigger for me. Thanks to those few car accidents I've experienced, they have developed an association of danger for me. When I must travel and my stressors may be high, I will carpool with a friend or family member. If I am left with no ride, I order an

Uber. I know when I'm stressed, I must take precautions with my triggers to avoid panic.

Parenting my children at home can cause high stress. Their restlessness can trigger anxiousness in me, so I incorporate more play time outside or organized activities inside. I'll even give some extra screen time for a mental break for me. There are answers to our problems; we just have to seek them out, find what works, use them diligently, and be not afraid to ask for help. ("Trust in the Lord with all your heart, and do not lean on your own understanding. In all your ways acknowledge Him, and He will make straight your paths." -*Proverbs 3:5-6*)

- **Exercise.** Exercise produces endorphins, which are chemicals in the brain that act as natural pain killers[4]. Endorphins improve sleep and reduce stress. They trigger the release of serotonin, norepinephrine, and dopamine — the primary neurochemicals responsible for helpful outcomes in pharmaceutical therapy. So, go outside with your family and get moving! Not only are you preventing triggers, but you are producing natural endorphins to ease stress and make sleeping easier. ("Beloved, I pray that all may go well with you and that you may be in good health, as it goes well with your soul." *-3 John 1:2*)

- **Journal your thoughts.** Jot down your worries as a written prayer to God. Not only can you reflect back on your journey as a testimony to others, but you are diligently taking time for yourself in a therapeutic manner[5]. Refer to pages 226-231 for examples. We all need an outlet for stress and worries, whether talking with a trusted person, or a form of exercise. Coupling multiple forms of therapy will be building blocks to support healthy actions in your mental health journey. ("Finally brothers, whatever is true, honorable, just, pure, lovely, commendable, if there is any excellence, if there is anything worthy of praise, think about these things." *-Philippians 4:8*)

- **Pray.** Above all else, pray. In the quiet moments, give thanksgiving for that break no matter how few those may be. In the utter chaos of raising tiny humans, seek the good in it. It's okay to admit you're struggling, and there are days where you want to quit. You are not alone. Pray through the hardship and struggle, claiming victory over what *seems* as a losing battle. If your battle was lost that day, remember *the war isn't lost*. Keep your head up, you've got this! ("Therefore I tell you, whatever you ask in prayer, believe that you have received it, and it will be yours." -*Mark 11:24*)

What's one method listed above you feel may be the hardest to practice in your day-to-day living? Why?

What's one method listed above you feel may be the easiest to practice in your day-to-day living? Why?

How can you implement a few of these in your daily life?

My daily wrestling with disordered and destructive thinking is a meticulous process I'd like to think of as "trusting the unseen". Implementing practical techniques and peace-filled Scripture are the two sacred key points in my map of navigation amongst stormy waters. When I fight against the raging sea of lies I've been told, by myself or others, I am trusting the light of truth the Father has laid out in front for me. When I fail, I find myself yet again trapped in a vicious cycle, reminding me of a damaging hurricane—the same kind of hurricane I experienced firsthand right before my fourteenth birthday in August of 2004.

When I fight against the raging sea of lies I've been told, by myself or others, I am trusting the light of truth the Father has laid out in front for me.

My father and I were sitting together on the couch, watching The Weather Channel. Eyeing the green, yellow, and red storm bands roll in from the Gulf of Mexico over to the southwest Florida coastline became a therapeutic ritual we grew to love and share. To the left of the bands we could see an animated swirling circle with wings the meteorologists had placed on a green screen. They were tracking the latest tropics the gulf had to offer—Hurricane Charley.

"It looks like Hurricane Charley is making a swift 90 degree right turn, shifting its course from Tampa to Punta Gorda", exclaimed the meteorologist, "Charlotte County folks, hunker down, he's coming your way in 30 minutes!"

In my innocence I had no idea what was before us. My father on the other hand bolted out of the seat, running to tell my mother the sudden turn of events. Seeing his panic startled my spirit instantly.

Before I knew it my brother and I were sheltered in my parents' walk-in closet, comforted with a few blankets, snacks, water bottles, and a pair of flashlights. The lights went first, and the light coming from our few flashlights were hardly comforting. I could hear my mother praying next to us, and I grew curious as to what was happening outside of our dark, small space. I snuck out of our protected corner because curiosity got the best of me. Seeing my dad use all of his strength to nail our dining room table to a blown out window and the sound of a freight train amplified, what seemed like 100 times, were the last moments of my memory from that event.

The damage in the aftermath was more than I could comprehend. If you are a 90's child like I am, you may remember a scene from the movie "Jumanji" with Robin Williams—towards the end of the movie, Alan Parrish and three other characters play the jungle-themed game inside the Parrish mansion. Thanks to the fate of the dice, the deep jungle comes alive inside the home, filling every nook and cranny with vines and ruin. That, my friend, is what Hurricane Charley left us with— every inch of our home filled with whatever outside jungle my neighborhood possessed.

That is the type of ruin that can take over when we allow such a vicious cycle to ruminate over our lives.

The Cycle of Worry

This damaging thought process is called the "*Cycle of Worry*"[6]. It begins on a path of anxiety, making it feel impossible to break. We focus so much on what troubles us we choose a *negative action as a defense mechanism*. When we live in turmoil in our mind, we long for wholeness and peace. We can feel trapped in the Cycle of Worry, and it can feel impossible to break it. In the Old Testament, Isaiah 9:6 names Jesus the Prince of Peace and "wonderful divine Counselor".

In the New Testament Paul writes to the church of Ephesus in Ephesians 2:14 reaffirming Isaiah's words that Jesus *is* our Peace.

"Peace I leave with you; my peace I give to you. Not as the world gives do I give to you. Let not your hearts be troubled, neither let them be afraid." *-John 14:27*

When we walk this Cycle of Worry out, we are bringing awareness to our minds, giving room for the cycle to be broken. We can see the end result (negative behavior) and work towards shifting our thinking to produce a positive behavior. Physically writing down what triggers us, following the path of what we feel, how our body reacts, and how we respond allows us to counteract the negative cycle with positive responses. Instead of letting our anxious thoughts and feelings be the driving force of our behavior, we can learn to slow the process down and respond in a healthy way.

Follow the Cycle of Worry example and fill in your own trigger on the next page to walk out what your Cycle of Worry looks like:

THE CYCLE OF WORRY

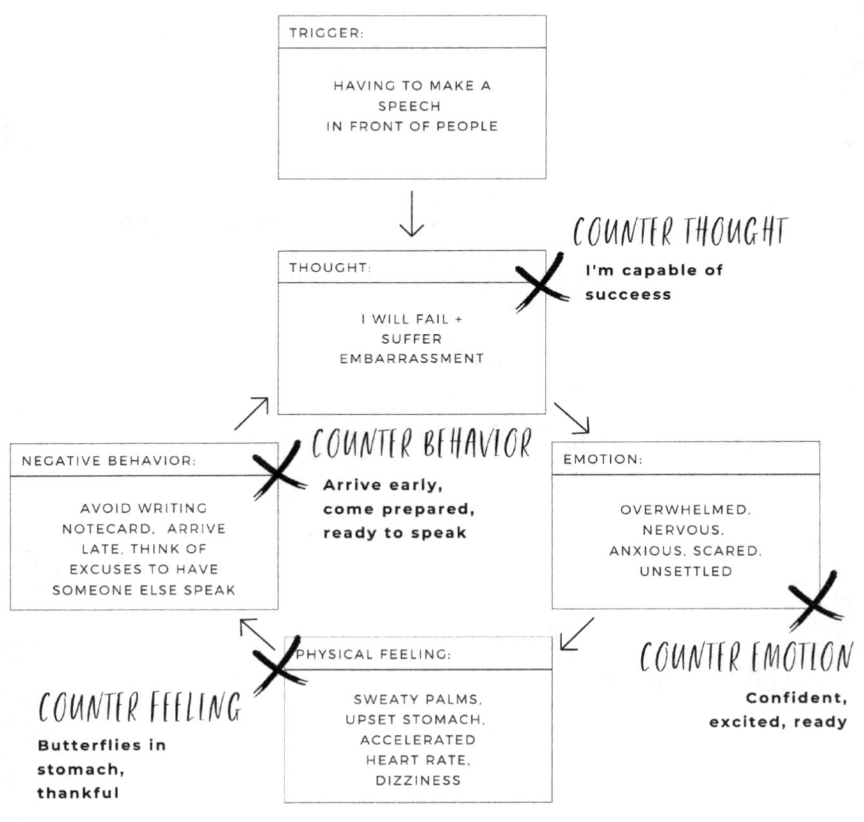

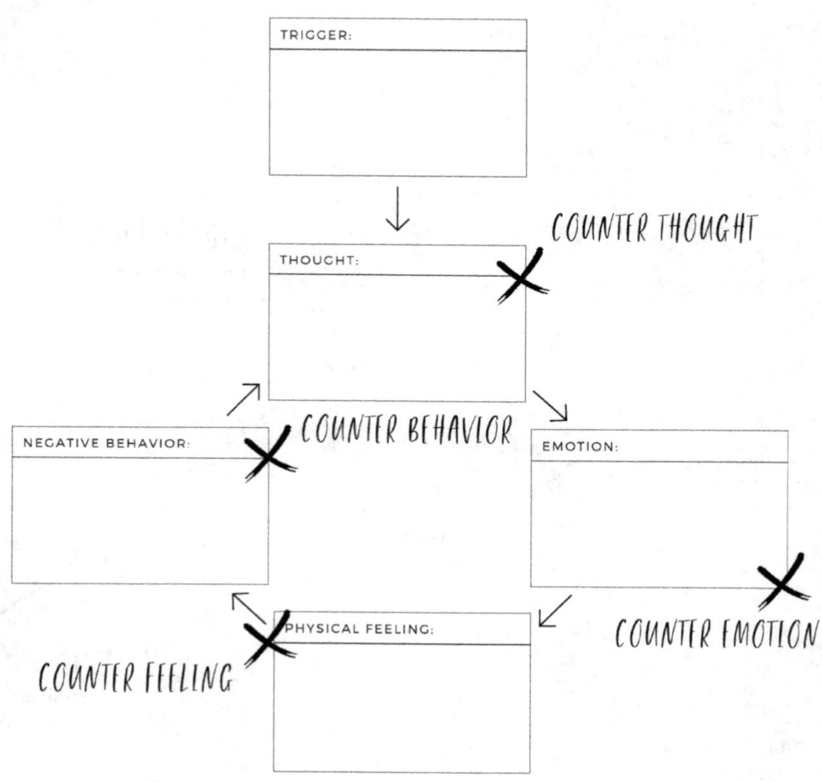
TRIGGER:
THOUGHT:
COUNTER THOUGHT
COUNTER BEHAVIOR
NEGATIVE BEHAVIOR:
EMOTION:
COUNTER EMOTION
PHYSICAL FEELING:
COUNTER FEELING

Jesus is able to give us peace because He *is* peace. In Mark 4, Jesus calms the raging seas by His command demonstrating His divine authority. Only God the Creator can calm the wind and sea. That same authority is the same mighty power that can calm the chaos in us.

That same authority is the same mighty power that can calm the chaos in us.

This *relief* He so freely gives banishes fear and sorrow from the heart because He is Sovereign. Understanding that He is in control can release us from circumstances we simply cannot control- if we allow our inner turmoil to accept it. We no longer have to be bound by the disorder inside because we have been reconciled in Jesus...we just have to walk in it.

When we surrender to His presence, we are giving ourselves the ability to live in His peace. He already gave us permission to live in it, we just need to act.

Control Issue

My anxiety stemmed from the fear of losing control. Once I realized I have no control over what is presented in from of me, the anxiety slowly started to lift. I learned that I needed to relinquish this illusion of control I thought I had, for the sake of my peace of mind! I have responsibility, but not control. I have the responsibility over how I respond, but not control over every situation.

We can control our actions, but His Sovereignty can work through our actions. God invites us to,

"Come to me, all who labor and are heavy laden, and I will give you rest. Take my yoke upon you, and learn from me, for I am gentle and lowly in heart, and you will find rest for your souls. For my yoke is easy, and my burden is light." -*Matthew 11:28-30*

I am not saying our struggles disappear altogether, but when we align our steps with His steps, we have the Ultimate Companion to carry our burdens. We need to release the desire of control back into His hands.

This was one of the hardest lessons I had to learn! Maybe like myself, you grew up with the saying,

"*You can control how you react, but not what was given to you.*"

It's the same principle. We have influence over our thoughts and actions, but not over the situations presented to us. We cannot control what thoughts pop into our head, but we can control what we do with them. Will we manifest the thought, or cast the lie out like He instructs us to?

We cannot control what thoughts pop into our head, but we can control what we do with them.

In the storm of anxiety, He is steady. We cannot predict what will happen next, but we can rely on God's consistency. *Will you choose to rely on His direction, casting away every destructive lie so that you can flourish as a Christ-follower? You will have to fight for it, but in the fight you're not alone—and you can do it.*

Which areas in your life do you find the easiest to surrender completely to Him?

List a few areas in your life you know you need to release over for Him to control, yet struggle to do so:

Lord, I pray that as we continue to learn how to work out the worries of our present and future, we continue to grow closer to You. I pray that whether we are new to the faith, or grew up in the church, there is something new to be learned in the old teachings. Amen.

WHEN WE GRACEFULLY NAVIGATE ANXIETY, WE ARE CHOOSING TO ALIGN OUR STEPS WITH HIS STEPS AS HE MINISTERS TO OUR MINDS

CHAPTER SIX

Fight to Flourish

"For freedom Christ has set us free; **stand firm** therefore, and do not submit again to a yoke of slavery." -*Galatians 5:1*

Before obediently walking under His guidance, I tried to be my own hero. Looking back, my lack of progress only confirmed just how much I needed Him— in prayer, calming practices, and mundane activities. I shifted, and with His power, began to gracefully navigate my anxiety, *continuously*, in seasons of joy, sorrow, motherhood, and pandemics (Hello, 2020!).

> "And my God will supply every need of yours according to His riches in glory in Christ Jesus" -*Philippians 4:19*

God is faithful to meet the need, but we must follow the choice we made with action. *James 2:20* tells us that faith without works is useless. Work looks like listening to the body He gave us, and being proactive to take care of it. It looks like intentionally resting in His provision, trusting He will guide us with a blueprint, and walking it out.

Staying proactive in your mental health and seeking Jesus daily is vital. Stress won't disappear. We have to fight to flourish. We can not escape from tragedies and pain, but with Jesus we can fight to be less anxious. With Jesus, we can walk as a people in the restoration process of freedom, because it is for freedom that Christ has set us free.

We are set free, permitted to flourish in His grace.

We are no longer under the penalty of sin.
We are set free, permitted to flourish in His grace.

Paul writes to the Christians in Galatia that they no longer have to abide by the law of Moses because of Jesus. He tells them it is through His blood they have been redeemed and set free. Not only are they set free from the law, but more importantly the consequences of sin—the second death. If they accepted this free gift of salvation, they would spend eternity in Heaven with Him, free of sin and shame. They no longer would be bound by the law of their society, but be able to flourish in the goodness of God's grace.

We, like the Galatians, are also no longer burdened by the yoke of slavery in our own lives. We can give ourselves permission to break free from the lie that our faith is lacking because our minds may be, because God first gave us the freedom to do so. We are released from the burdens of struggling alone because God is on our side bringing light into the darkness, and order to the chaos.

We've been given the gift of 'choice'. When we choose to do life in the Spirit, He empowers us to flourish and bear good fruit for the sake of peace, and His glory.

What does it look like to *flourish in anxiety?*

Flourishing looks like walking into a crowded room, timid, but choosing to stay. It's taking on bigger dreams and projects with Christ-like confidence, when before, the thought alone scared you enough to prohibit action. It's turning to post-it notes filled with Scripture in a moment of panic instead of allowing the worst-case scenarios to ruminate in your mind.

It's giving yourself grace daily because God gives it to you. Even when you take two steps back after making a giant leap forward, you know you will prevail and step forward again.

It's understanding you fight silent battles no one else knows about, but God does. He gets into the battered boat with you and navigates the storm of anxiety with you. You are able to see the raging waves and your first initial reaction isn't fear, but hope, because you know you are not alone in the journey.

Take some time to write down the verses shared so far - maybe on a sticky note, I personally love those, and tape to your mirror or some type of vision board. It's important for us to reflect back on them during our times of fear and anxiety.

Transform That Mind!

Do you remember this saying from childhood, "*What goes in, must come out*"?

The phrase isn't just food and water. What we feed our mind and spirit will ultimately come out in our speech and actions. If I want to lead an uplifted life, I need to speak positivity to myself and others because God instructs me to do so. If I want to have a joyful attitude, I must seek out things that bring joy and count hidden markings of His joy in the ruin. If I yearn to give grace to my children, then I need to come to the Father asking for grace to fill me so I can pour it out. If I want a holy confidence, I must understand God created me on purpose and for a purpose.

If I yearn to give grace to my children, then I need to come to the Father asking for grace to fill me so I can pour it out.

Our mind is a powerful tool. We go where our thoughts take us as they define our actions.

Where are your thoughts steering you?

We know too well how this plays out in the online world. Thanks to social media, we fall into the comparison game more than any other generation. We fill our minds with false, filtered truth. We take in negativity and doubts from those tiny squares. Want more peace in life? Limit your time on social media, and spend time with your family. Shift your focus from the trivial things of life, like the content online, to what matters— this will produce lasting peace in a negative world.

His desire for us is to be so intimately involved with Him, that we choose His joy in any circumstance.

The more negativity you allow in your life, the more those thoughts will become a stronghold. A *stronghold* hinders our ability to seek and live out optimism in our day-to-day[1]. It also hinders the greatest opportunity of all: *to live our life to the fullest as God intended*. His desire for us is to be so intimately involved with Him, that we *choose* His joy in any circumstance.

God intends for us to live life mirroring His love, enjoying the grace and peace attained through seeking Him daily. Our *devastating* thinking will hold us captive, *dictating* our feelings, which will then lead to a *destructive* action.

Our negative thinking and destructive actions may push those closest to us out of our lives. We become consumed with bitterness, frustration, irritation, and blame. Don't allow your mind to rob you of the joy of the people in your life. We are not meant to do this alone— choose to stay in circles that can protect you. Choose to fight those cognitive distortions that your people "don't want you", because they do *need* you.

Our devastating thinking will hold us captive, dictating our feelings, which will then lead to a destructive action.

Cognitive Distortions

There is a term in psychology for the lies we think and the scenarios we make up, all based on false information. An inaccurate and negatively biased thought is called a *Cognitive Distortion*[2]. These thoughts are the lies of our lives (as stated at the start of this book); lies we have been given since the beginning of time.

Genesis 3:1-13 says, "*Now the serpent was more crafty than any other beast of the field that the Lord God had made. He said to the woman, "Did God actually say, 'You shall not eat of any tree in the garden'?" And the woman said to the serpent, "We may eat of the fruit of the trees in the garden, but God said, 'You shall not eat of the fruit of the tree that is in the midst of the garden, neither shall you touch it, lest you die.'" But the serpent said to the woman, "You will not surely die. For God knows that when you eat of it your eyes will be opened, and you will be like God, knowing good and evil." So when the woman saw that the tree was good for food, and that it was a delight to the eyes, and that the tree was to be desired to make one wise, she took of its fruit and ate, and she also gave some to her husband who was with her, and he ate. Then the eyes of both were opened, and they knew that they were naked. And they sewed fig leaves together and made themselves loincloths. And they heard the sound of the Lord God walking in the garden in the cool of the day, and the man and his wife hid themselves from the presence of the Lord God among the trees of the garden. But the Lord God called to the man and said to him, "Where are you?" And he said, "I heard the sound of you in the garden, and I was afraid, because I was naked, and I hid myself." He said, "Who told you that you were naked? Have you eaten of the tree of which I commanded you not to eat?" The man said, "The woman whom you gave to be with me, she gave me fruit of the tree, and I ate." Then the Lord God said to the woman, "What is this that you have done?" The woman said, "The serpent deceived me, and I ate."*

Whew.

Satan is conniving and his lies are desirable and believable. He gives them packaged as the truth, making it logical and endearing, distorting and calling into question God's Word. Eve fell for it. Her act of disobedience from being deceived altered everything for us. Our imperfect bodies and minds are a result of The Fall, all because of a lie she believed.

Our imperfect bodies and minds are a result of The Fall, all because of a lie she believed.

Satan wants nothing more than to separate us from the love of God, and His truth for our lives because he has always wanted to destroy God's creation. Since the moment Satan decided to elevate himself above God, his agenda is to destroy anything and everything representing God. Just as he deceived Eve, he is taking the truth today and tweaking it just enough to deceive our thinking, making us believe it is The Truth.

It is imperative we learn who God is and what His Word says, so that we may flourish in recognizing false statements when we hear them. We can distinguish between what is true and what is *disguised* as truth.

So what are some basic ways we *distort our thinking*[3]?

- **All or Nothing:** Everything is black or white.
  - You focus on one side more than the other, known as *splitting*. For example, when/if you fail, you see yourself as a complete failure. You think of the glass being half-empty, instead of half-full.

- **Over-Generalization:** Seeing a single, negative event as a never-ending pattern of defeat.
    - For example, experiencing a relationship with a narcissistic individual can lead you to believe everyone is like that, therefore you avoid relationships altogether. You may also believe that since you were an anxious child, you are doomed to live the rest of your life as an anxious adult.

- **Mental Filter:** You dwell on one single negative detail only. Your focus of all reality is distorted and darkened.
    - You are filtering out all of the positive, or “silver linings”, in a situation, leading to higher levels of anxiety and depression.

- **Disqualifying the Positive:** Any positive experience in your life you automatically reject and "don't count".
    - You look at your life as if you possess a black cloud over it, dismissing any good that is given to you.

- You disqualify any given opportunity because you feel unworthy to receive it. *It must be for someone else.*

- **Jumping to Conclusions:**
  - You choose a negative interpretation, even though the facts of the situation are not final to support your interpretation.

- **Magnification or Minimization:** Exaggerating the importance of things, or diminishing things until they appear tiny and unimportant.
  - This often connects with disqualifying the positive, because on one side, you dismiss the positive and downsize it. On the other, you exaggerate the black cloud hovering over you. The consequences of your mistakes disqualifies any/all good in your life.

- **Emotional Reasoning**: If I feel it, it MUST be true.
  - When you feel inadequate, you decide you are a worthless person. When overwhelmed looking at your to-do list, you feel it is impossible to

tackle, so you do nothing. You justify your actions, because you are *trusting your gut*, making it true. In some cases, trusting our gut works. However, they are not always accurate.

- "**Should**" **Statements**: Trying to motivate yourself that you *should* do it, ought to be able to do it.
    - When you direct these statements towards yourself and others, you feel guilt, anger, and frustration. When a healthy moral or principle becomes an internal *rule*, it can create a problem. Instead of having a guideline, we steer towards the side of *feeling righteous*, or like a failure, because what *should* happen. If you have a fear of flying, and notice the fear is gradually getting worse over the years, you start repeating this statement to yourself: "I should be able to fly with no issue, after all, I am an adult now! I ought to be able to fly with no anxiety!" Over time this only creates more stress and disappointment with unreasonable pressure on yourself.

- **Labeling & Mislabeling**: Attaching a negative label to yourself, such as "I am so dumb; I am a loser".
   - When you feel incompetent, you don't push yourself to do anything because you believe you are not able. This also applies when labeling someone else when their behavior angers you.

- **Personalization**: Seeing yourself as the cause of a negative event, when in fact, you were not the primary cause.
   - Imagine you invited a group of friends out to a restaurant or a concert. If they ended up hating the food, or not liking the band, you think you are the cause because it was your idea. You then stop making any suggestions for fear of rejection and *your fault* scenarios.

Let's identify the ways we distort our thinking through our own cognitive distortions:

IDENTIFYING **COGNITIVE DISTORTION**

A LIE, INACCURATE, OR NEGATIVELY BIASED THOUGHT.

COGNITIVE DISTORTION:	COUNTER-THOUGHT:
☐ MY HUSBAND IS LATE FROM WORK, HE MUST HAVE HAD A BAD CAR ACCIDENT.	☐ TRAFFIC MIGHT BE BAD, APPOINTMENT MAY HAVE RAN LATE, BUT HE IS SAFE.
☐ I CAN'T MANAGE A SIMPLE SCHEDULE, THEREFORE I AM A FAILURE.	☐ I HAVE STRENGTHS AND WEAKNESSES, BUT I AM NOT A FAILURE. I AM SEEN AND LOVED BY GOD.
☐	☐
☐	☐
☐	☐

YOU ARE SEEN. YOU ARE VALUED. YOU ARE LOVED.

Satan's lies or what someone else has said about you is not who you are. The worst thought *you* have created in your mind about yourself does not define you. God defines you, and He alone, for He is the one who created you. of it.

The worst thought you have created in your mind about yourself does not define you. God defines you, and He alone, for He is the one who created you.

When circumstances don't go our way, pain introduces itself in our lives, or when we are paralyzed with fear in a moment, God walks it out with us. The goal is to get to a point that we can say,

"Lord, ***even if*** *this situation is not ideal, I trust Your hand is at work in it. I trust Your guidance and walk in your grace."*

When we practice walking out the "even if" scenario rather than focusing on the "what if" possibilities, we are actively pursuing a faith-filled life, opposing a fear-driven life. Can you counter your cognitive distortion to walk out an "even if" life? ***What does this look like for you?***

WORKING OUT THE "WHAT IFS"

THE WHAT IF SCENARIO:	HOW LIKELY WILL THIS OCCUR?	BEST-CASE SCENARIO?
MY PLANE WOULD CRASH AND I WOULD DIE, LEAVING BEHIND MY CHILDREN AND FAMILY	1 IN 3.37 BILLION CHANCE OF DYING IN A COMMERCIAL AIRPLANE CRASH 98.6% OF CRASHES DO NOT RESULT IN FATALITY	IF PLANE CRASHES, THE CHANCES OF SURVIVAL ARE HIGHLY FAVORABLE
WORST-CASE IF IT HAPPENS?	**HOW WOULD I COPE IF IT HAPPENS?**	**WHAT ARE THE FACTS?**
I DIE AND WOULD FINALLY MEET JESUS FACE TO FACE. CHILDREN WOULD BE TAKEN CARE OF	IF I SURVIVE THE CRASH, I HAVE TRUSTED LOVED ONES IN MY CORNER TO HELP ME THROUGH THE TRAUMA	18% OF PEOPLE SUFFER FROM THE FEAR OF FLYING. I AM NOT ALONE IN THIS FEAR. MY CHANCES OF CRASHING ARE EXTREMELY LOW

OVERESTIMATING THE:

- LIKELIHOOD OF AN EVENT
- AWFULNESS OF AN EVENT

AND *UNDERESTIMATION* OF OUR ABILITY
TO COPE WITH THE EVENT
IS CALLED ***CATASTROPHIZING***.

THE WHAT IF SCENARIO:	HOW LIKELY WILL THIS OCCUR?	BEST-CASE SCENARIO?
WORST-CASE IF IT HAPPENS?	**HOW WOULD I COPE IF IT HAPPENS?**	**WHAT ARE THE FACTS?**

THE WHAT IF SCENARIO:	HOW LIKELY WILL THIS OCCUR?	BEST-CASE SCENARIO?

WORST-CASE IF IT HAPPENS?	HOW WOULD I COPE IF IT HAPPENS?	WHAT ARE THE FACTS?

DECATASTROPHIZATION IS TO ADDRESS THESE *COGNITIVE DISTORTIONS*, ASKING QUESTIONS THAT LEAD DOWN THE "WHAT-IF" PATH. USING THIS TECHNIQUE WILL HELP YOU EVALUATE HOW LIKELY YOUR THOUGHTS ARE TO BE TRUE. WHEN WE ARE ABLE TO LOOK AT THE SITUATION RATIONALLY, WE OFTEN FIND THAT THESE ANXIOUS THOUGHTS ARE NOT BASED ON REALITY.

Until the day I meet Jesus face-to-face, I must focus on what is happening right now. He doesn't want me to just look up at the sky and wait for His return. He doesn't want me to look ahead with worry or sit on the sorrow of yesterday. No. To flourish I need to act right here and now, because no matter what situation arises, I need to start today by being more present and *accepting of the now*. By doing so, I am practicing *mindfulness*.

Mindfulness[4] is *not* a silencing of the mind, but *being aware of yourself and your surroundings*. It is not exclusively an activity that is calming/peaceful, or subduing negative thoughts. It is also focusing on the sensory observations: what you hear, smell, feel, see, instead of the *why* and *how*. Being aware of the present can help you overcome and cope with the unhealthy thoughts that produce anxiety, such as imagining worst-case scenarios for future situations.

Mindfulness can *improve your quality of life* by training you to savor the good as it comes. It can improve your mental health by giving you the tools to deal with the negativity in your life. It invites reflection and forgiveness as you let go of situations out of your control. It reduces stress and enhances focus, giving the task at hand your full attention.

"Do not be conformed to this world, but be transformed by the renewal of your mind, that by testing you may discern what is the will of God, what is good and acceptable and perfect." -*Romans 12:2*

How to practice Mindfulness[5]:

- **Time**. Find a comfortable, quiet place to sit or lay down. For some of you, waking up before everyone else in your house is ideal.

  If you're like me, I work best in the late morning while my kids are doing school work or having a brain break by playing outside. Whether it's in the morning, afternoon or evening, find just 10 minutes where you can be left alone. Mothers, especially those of you with young children like myself, I hear you. It feels nearly impossible to be left alone for a minute, let alone 10 minutes. Compromise with your spouse, if need be, for them to be with the children while you find a quiet space for this small time-frame for yourself. Single parents, try this while they are asleep. You are worth the alone time.

- **Focus.** Now that you're alone, close your eyes and focus on what you feel in the quiet. You may need to wear headphones to drown out the noise in your home. Hone in on the sensations you are feeling. What do you feel/smell/hear? Are you feeling anxious, or calm? Don't reflect on why, but simply feel.

- **Breathe.** Take slow, deep breaths. This will also help if you find yourself in the middle of a panicked moment. Focus on your breathing and how it feels to slowly inhale and exhale. Calm your heart rate, and relax in this moment.

- **Wander to Guidance.** Your mind may wander, and to be expected. Allow it for a couple minutes, then, guide your focus back to your breathing.

- **Repeat.** Continue this process as long as you can.

As Christ-followers, we are instructed to take every thought captive (*2 Cor 10:5*), practice God-honoring thoughts (*Phil 4:9*), and use prayer as a biblical method of mindfulness, giving thanks in all circumstances (*1 Thes 5:17-18*).

Take this time to *direct your focus into His presence*. Put on some soothing worship in the background, and continue the steps *Focus* through *Repeat*. Practicing mindfulness through a biblical approach can help shift our mindset from weary thoughts, to the calming markings of His presence.

Will you choose to see yourself as He sees you, opening your eyes to His markings of joy in your life?

Lord, teach us to walk in Your peace to calm the battles of our mind. Our lives feel in utter chaos, and we need You to be the calming center of it. Thank You for Your forgiveness that brings all peace and understanding in our lives. Teach us, as we face daily obstacles, to be peacemakers in them, and for our attention to be directly focused on You. Amen.

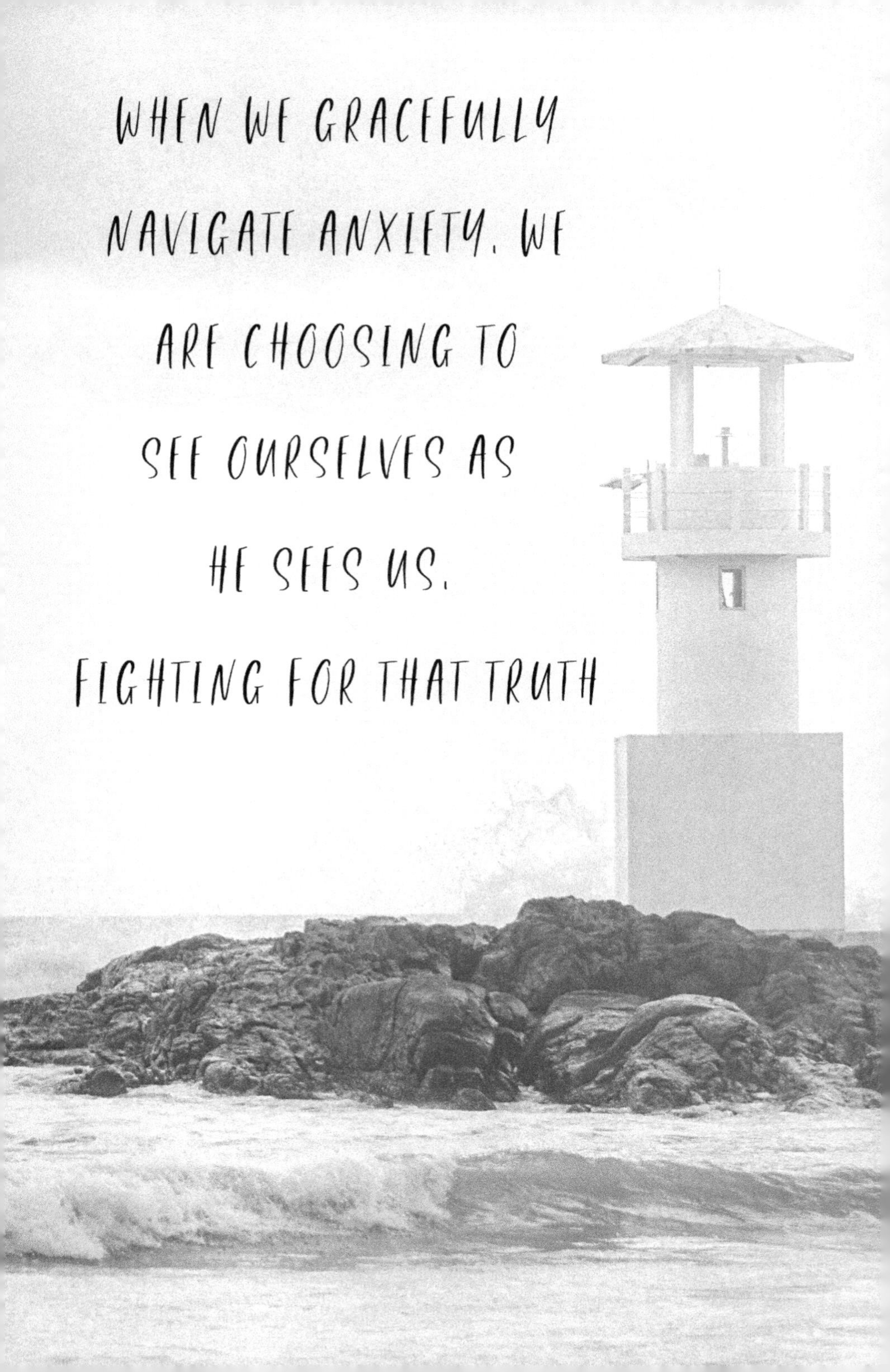
WHEN WE GRACEFULLY
NAVIGATE ANXIETY, WE
ARE CHOOSING TO
SEE OURSELVES AS
HE SEES US.
FIGHTING FOR THAT TRUTH

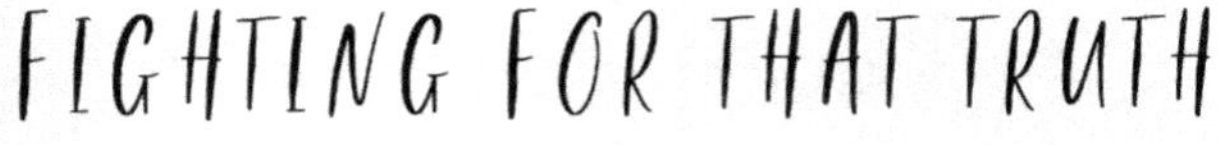

CHAPTER SEVEN

Markings of Joy

"You make known to me the path of life; **in your presence there is fullness of joy**; at your right hand are pleasures forevermore." *-Psalm 16:11*

I'm a visual person. It's not enough for me to hear the message and receive it. I have to look at it and meditate on it. Sometimes I have to read a sentence over and over to retain the information. Unfortunately, this is why audio books hardly serve me. The overall message may stick, but the intricate details won't. I remember a phrase from a camp counselor in my youth group days, "God cares about the details in our lives, and we should too." What was once an annoying ounce of optimism displayed in this beaming counselor has now transferred over into my sanctification process of graceful navigation. Rather than being spiteful of my current situation, be it a newly homeschooling mom or having to retire from my beloved career of photography, I have to deliberately choose to seek out the good in it.

So, I write down details that I can reflect back on and not to let them pass me by. It's easy to see the gloom and doom when that's all you're focusing on. We need to practice writing down the wins, or the *joy* in our lives, so that we can practice reflecting on that more.

> *Physically seeing the good in your life on paper will help shift your negative, biased thinking to gratitude.*

Physically seeing the good in your life on paper will help shift your negative, biased thinking to gratitude and truth. When you make an attempt to be mindful of the good and document it, you see the positive more than the negative.

I pray that you take these opportunities and write down the wins in the thick of it, so that you may look back and see where God was in your valley. We get to know God more intimately in the valleys, so do not despise them. When we are left with nothing else but to abide in His presence, we are gifted with His markings of joy. Instead of allowing the hardship of the valley to swallow us whole, we can choose to deepen our relationship with the Father. After all, if God wastes nothing, why should we?

When our minds focus on the, "What will this cost?" scenario, it tends to far outweigh the endgame, which is, "What will I gain from it?" Give God permission to be the potter molding the clay in you. He can transform you in ways you cannot imagine.

We have the choice to allow Him to teach us, and give ourselves permission to count it all joy regardless of the circumstance. Let God in His sovereignty direct your journey, and then be a light to others who need it.

Sometimes what we write are simple pleasures we find in our day-to-day. We can easily spot them because they bring instant joy, no matter the circumstance of the day. They are little gifts given by the Father, because He delights in the joy of His children. As parents we delight in giving good, simple gifts to our children. God's heart is the same but in a greater capacity.

My son is the pure image of his father, from his personality, to his baby blue eyes and chin. Apart from his nose, eyelashes, and lips—those are mine. Like my husband, I am learning he is a "words of affirmation" kind of guy at just six years old. I delight in his compassion and thoughtfulness; pair that with his silliness and whit, he effortlessly shows to anyone he meets how much he wears his heart on his sleeve.

Back to when he attended school in person, I loved hiding little love notes for him inside his lunchbox. I'd write uplifting phrases on post-its, short and sweet for his then five-year-old comprehension, all over his bedroom door and walls. I knew reading loving words from his mama would bring joy and instantly lift his spirits., no matter what kind of day he had. As simple and effortless my gesture was, it developed confidence in his tiny world.

Never underestimate this power of a simple moment. We so easily miss the gifts such as these given by the Father because we are too distracted by the hardship of our day. If I, as Hudson's mommy, can leave little gifts for him to find joy in, how much more can my Heavenly Father leave around for me to delight in?

You may enjoy a hot cup of coffee in the morning while basking in the silence of your home before everyone wakes. I do enjoy a hot cup of coffee in the silence, reading a devotion. I take note of what brings me joy, and I reflect back at the opportunities He freely gave me to replenish my soul in the valley. I see His markings of joy, and it brings me comfort and hope for the future.

On the following pages, I provide space for you to write down His Markings of Joy for each month:

MARKINGS OF JOY

JANUARY

FEBRUARY

MARCH

APRIL

MAY

JUNE

YEAR:

ACHIEVEMENTS

JULY

AUGUST

SEPTEMBER

OCTOBER

NOVEMBER

DECEMBER

YEAR:

Filling Your Cup

What we are doing at home for our families is holy work. Our children need a happy, healthy mother just as much as our spouse needs a healthy wife. Our friends need a healthy confidante to turn to when their own world is crashing. At first we may view this self-care list as selfish, but please understand, *taking care of yourself is as selfless as it comes, because you will be happier and recharged to pour yourself into your loved ones.*

I like how The Message Translation of this Roman's passage conveys Paul's writing:

"Don't burn out; keep yourselves fueled and aflame. Be alert servants of the Master, cheerfully expectant. Don't quit in hard times; pray all the harder. Help needy Christians; be inventive in hospitality." *-Romans 12:11-13*

Celebrate the wins by capturing the examples of His joy here and in a journal. Every detail is accounted for, and yes, He sees it all! Actively seek Him in your day-to-day fights with the troubles in your mind.

There cannot be a victory without a battle, and we cannot be conquerors if we don't participate in the fight, under His guidance. Don't quit or falter. Pour back into yourself to avoid burnout. Take comfort in knowing that when you fail to do so, He is able to do what we cannot.

Won't He do it?

On the following page you will find a list to fill out attainable, easy-to-achieve tasks that will help *fill your cup*. Whatever relieves stress for you, write it down. If seeing fresh flowers in a vase brightens your day, buy a beautiful bouquet. If reading alone with a candle soothes your soul, write that down and put it into action. Take that list and put it on your mirror or refrigerator, to remind yourself to fill your cup up often.

Activities that fill my cup are independent, as time alone restores my soul. Whether it's alone time in my bedroom studying, listening to worship music, or walking around a store solo; both are nurturing grounds for me to take a break.

I know you've heard this before,

"*We can't pour from an empty cup.*"

We can rest in the Father, relying on Him to pour from His abundance. As we pour out, He pours in. The more He pours in, the more we pour out.

Doing good work is emptying our cup so that He can fill it. Sometimes, that looks like little gifts from the Father, like simple activities to restore us once more.

FILL YOUR CUP

"LORD, I EMPTY MY CUP SO THAT YOU CAN FILL IT."

I FEEL DRAINED WHEN...

My cup overflows with your blessing.

PSALM 23:5

I'M GRATEFUL FOR:

SMALL ACTIVITIES TO FILL MY CUP:

- [ ]
- [ ]
- [ ]
- [ ]
- [ ]
- [ ]

PRAYER REQUESTS:

As you have learned to identify what your anxiety looks like, what triggers it, and practical ways to cope with it, the next step is to live it out. As you learn to embrace who you are, and affirm He created you on purpose, it will be important for you to come back to the prompts in this section. The work is never done until we are finally face-to-face with our glorious Savior, and what a wonderful day that will be!

Until then, life changes, and we hope to grow for the better. Reflecting on who you were, and how far you've come, is your testimony to help and inspire others.

And hey, it's okay if your track record is messy.

God didn't use perfect people to fulfill His purpose. Their imperfections made an impact, and ours can too - for our loved ones, and even those we haven't met yet.

Rahab in the book of Joshua was a prostitute and a traitor to her own people. She recognized God was the one True God, and so He restored her, making her a part of the lineage of Jesus.

Gideon in Judges cowardly tried to look for any excuse to avoid the plans God had for his life. Yet, God still chose to use him to deliver the Israelites from the hands of the Midianites.

David in the book of Samuel was a shepherd boy turned King. Despite his lustful, adulterous, murderous tendencies, he too was added to the lineage of Christ.

Saul in the book of Acts persecuted Christians. He approved the killing of a disciple named Stephen, and diligently hunted for more Christ-followers. Later we learn his name changed to Paul because of his radical transformation because of God's saving grace. We know his writings today in Scripture through the books of 1 Thessalonians, Galatians, Philippians, Philemon, 1 and 2 Corinthians, Romans, and much more.

The list can go on because we have a wealth of history recorded in the living, breathing Word of God. They were loved, cared for, and used by Him. If He is the same yesterday, today, and forevermore—why can't He use me? You?

Will you allow your testimony of graceful navigation reach those that I may not be able to reach? Will you overcome the hardship we were promised in this life, knowing that even when it's hard, He is right there with you?

Lord, I pray that their progress becomes a great testimony to those around them. I pray that this book has given them hope, igniting a fire to help those around them. We know we cannot have a testimony without a test, and we cannot make an impact without imperfections. Teach us to humbly own our imperfections, because we are chosen to make an impact to amplify Your glory. Amen.

WHEN WE GRACEFULLY NAVIGATE ANXIETY, WE ARE CHOOSING TO SEE HIS MARKINGS OF JOY IN EVERY SEASON, NO MATTER HOW SMALL THEY APPEAR

CHAPTER EIGHT

Overcome

"Little children, you are from God and **have overcome them**, for **He who is in you is greater than he who is in the world**." *-1 John 4:4*

"I have said these things to you, that in me you may **have peace**. In the world you will have tribulation. But take heart; **I have overcome the world**." *-John 16:33*

It's been one year since the writing of *Gracefully Navigating Anxiety's* manuscript. As of today, and sixteen years after my first encounter with anxiety, I am not fully healed. I am, however, flourishing in His peace and grace as I continue to navigate whatever stormy waters lie ahead. Staying faithful to His teachings, engaging with uplifting Christ-followers, and spending intentional time with the Father is how I overcome. The joy from preserving will be worth it in the end.

What will it require for Christians to live life in faith, and not consumed by debilitating anxiety? Since we are marked by grace, given hope by the Father, and devoted to serve others, in the waiting we already have all that we need. In the waiting we have the answer of what the end looks like—fully restored in His presence.

I know that this battle is not just of flesh and blood, but against the rulers of the dark world and heavenly realms *(Eph 6:12)*. Whether we believe it or not, there is a war raged over our souls and our minds. When we ignore the hidden spiritual warfare occurring in both, we won't be alert to the enemy's attacks on our thoughts. If we aren't prepared mentally or spiritually, we will fail in the physical. Just as a soldier heads off to war wearing protective gear and equipped with weapons for the fight, we too need to be ready. We have the Ultimate Commander on our side, and we need to follow His instructions for our own protection and victory.

As we are fighting for the victory over our minds, daily, rest in the truth that the entire victory has already been won. Jesus conquered the grave with His death and resurrection. Death has been defeated, and through Him we can rest in that victory. So, while we may continue this struggle because of our sinful nature, we can give ourselves grace and receive His peace because the end has been foretold. In the end, we have the victory because it's already been settled. I don't know about you, but realizing this truth makes it a lot easier to receive His peace.

When your mind fails you, give yourself grace. Pick yourself back up, reassess with the people in your corner, and move forward. The path may not be easy, but the end is decided; and it is painted in victory.

Throughout this process you have been equipped with the knowledge of what is happening in your mind, how to handle it, and ways to practice spiritual mindfulness for peace. You must continue daily to answer this call:

The path may not be easy, but the end is decided; and it is painted in victory.

“Will I fight the worries of my mind and become a conqueror?”

“Will I choose truth and realize the negativity I’ve been manifesting are lies that will only destroy me?”

For every fear and hurt we experience, there is an **empty grave** that defeats the eternal sting of it. For every negative thought and judgement we put towards ourselves, grace covers it. His compassion through Scripture brings us joy when we actively seek it!

"When the cares of my heart are many, your consolations cheer my soul.” *-Psalm 94:19*

Dwell on the truth that the Cross gives— we were worth dying for because God loves us that much. He sees our thoughts and cares for us deeply in our damage. When our surroundings don't make sense, He makes sense in the midst of our confusion.

Choose Him. Choose your family. Choose your friends.

How?

Actively use the tools given to you.

Seek out a counselor if you need to.

Therapy isn't just for wounded people, it's for everyone.

Break the stigma that surrounds anxiety and make that appointment. Counseling can *help* you come to terms with your past, and thrive in the present.

Those of us that were once broken have great potential through Him to be masters at mending. Will you say "yes" to your process to serve others in theirs?

Refuse to sink, conqueror.

Prayer, His Word, and help from professionals and/or friends are key tools to help you stay afloat.

In the following pages you will find resources on how to find a local counselor and a church. Your mental health should have equal priority, with your spiritual and physical health. The three work in harmony to give you a flourishing life, if done intentionally and under His guidance. Just as we are encouraged to be proactive in our physical health, may we apply the same urgency to our relationship with Jesus and in our mental wellness. Involve your primary care physician in the process, so that they and your counselor can be on the same page in caring for you. Allow your trusted, and Biblically-sound, church members to walk with you so that you're not alone. Remember, Jesus is our Redeemer, Counselor, Healer, and Peace. He also uses His people in the process. Be proactive and set yourself up for success by saying "yes".

Our Great Helper

We all have a Helper in this life as Christians. Jesus sent the Holy Spirit to fight on our behalf while He prepares a place for us. He is the third, beautiful part of the Trinity: God the Father, Jesus the Son, and the Holy Spirit as the Helper.

"Nevertheless, I tell you the truth: it is to your advantage that I go away, for if I do not go away, **the Helper** will not come to you. But if I go, **I will send him to you**." *-John 16:7*

Jesus said it is to our advantage, for our *betterment*, that He leaves; for He is sending the Helper in His place. The Helper, **the Holy Spirit**, can help us actively differentiate between the Truth and the lies in our mind.

Jesus Christ is our *mediator*, becoming the ultimate reconciliation to God on our behalf.

"...that is, in Christ God was reconciling the world to himself, not counting their trespasses against them, and entrusting to us the message of reconciliation." *-2 Corinthians 5:19*

The Holy Spirit is our *intercessor*, praying on our behalf to God thanks to the redeeming work of Jesus.

"Likewise the Spirit helps us in our weakness. For we do not know what to pray for as we ought, but the Spirit himself intercedes for us with groanings *too deep for words*." *-Romans 8:26*

Rest easy, because you have Jesus going to the Father on your behalf. When we don't know what to pray for the Holy Spirit intercedes for you in prayer. The struggles we face in our mind? Our Helper is already bringing them to the Father on our behalf.

Remember: **You are more than a diagnosis**.

You are *chosen*.

You are *worthy*.

You are *loved*.

You are a **conqueror**.

"But thanks be to God, who gives us the victory through our Lord Jesus Christ. Therefore, my beloved brothers, be steadfast, immovable, always abounding in the work of the Lord, knowing that in the Lord your labor is not in vain." *-1 Corinthians 15:57-58*

"The Lord bless you and keep you; the Lord make His face to shine upon you and be gracious to you; the Lord lift up His countenance upon you and ***give you peace****." -Numbers 6:24-26*

WHEN WE GRACEFULLY
NAVIGATE ANXIETY, WE
ARE CHOOSING TO
SEE OUR TOUGHEST STORM
AND USE IT AS OUR
GREATEST STRENGTH

BONUS

You Need People

Make a list of names of those you consider to be "your people". These are the names of those you consider to be your support system. ***You'll find on page 197 I provided a chart for your list.***

Who shows up when everyone else leaves?

Who leaves you inspired and challenged to do/be better?

Looking back, those I would call "my people"would change. Just as much as seasons transitioned, I found the people I'd allow in my circle to come and go as well. Our lives would shift, and obedient "yes's" to the next chapter of our lives would play out. As one leaves for college or off to get married, another moves in from out of state.

The pace of our lives would hardly run the same race, and so, we said our goodbyes and kept in touch via social media. As painful as the "see you later was", it was okay.

Our time together in person served its purpose, and just as Paul said his goodbyes to his people, they cherished the time they had together. I'm thankful for the gift of social media and FaceTime video chats to see their faces, unlike our friend Paul. However, the sting of the physical departure remained the same. Each person has given so much joy in my life for the time they were present, and I hope I have done the same for them. The friendship wasn't counted as a loss or time wasted, rather, another healing piece to my broken puzzle.

I need people. I need community. You, too, need people and community. If you're an introvert like me, it can be so easy to believe the lie that we thrive in isolation. Again, friend Natalia's husband brought up a valid point, "Why do you think they put prisoners in isolation? There's no greater punishment than putting someone in isolation over a long period of time." We thrive in community, mirroring our Heavenly Father, Jesus the Son, and the Holy Spirit. Think of "your people" in this season and write their name down. Keep their names close so you can enlist them in your journey. Let them know their value in your life, and ask that they will consider to be a part of this "help line" you are creating.

Once your "people" are written down and are with you in the journey, ask them to hold you accountable in keeping safe guards active in your life. Perhaps you love to indulge in that night-cap daily, but you know it's not helping your walk with Jesus or your anxiety.

Ask that they hold you accountable in swapping out the night-cap for non-caffeinated hot tea.

Maybe you're like me and need a buddy system for travel to help ease anxiety. Ask someone to carpool if your schedules match.

If you experience social anxiety, ask someone to be your "ice breaker" in a crowd. Agree beforehand on a "safe word" for exiting, as a precaution if things get shaky. Baby steps.

What do you do if you don't have "your people"?

A friend of mine, Donnie, knows what you're going through. He has experienced anxiety, loneliness, and isolation for many years. Per his advice, reach out and "push" yourself into the circles you want to be involved in. Sometimes, the people you see at work or church might not know you are longing for personal community. In order to be seen sometimes, we need to be heard. Push past those lies and insecurities that you will be rejected and go for it!

You also need to know when to say 'no'. Safeguards protect your peace, but you have to intentionally set them in order for them to work. Figure out which "yes" brings you peace and challenges you in a healthy way. Saying "no'' to a devastating, triggering situation actually says "yes" to peace. Get involved with a community, but also protect your peace with intentionality and wisdom.

Safeguards protect your peace, but you have to intentionally set them in order for them to work.

YOU ARE MY PEOPLE.

YEAR:

NAME	FAVORITE QUALITY	MY PRAYER FOR THEM	WHY I TRUST THEM

YEAR:

NAME	FAVORITE QUALITY	MY PRAYER FOR THEM	WHY I TRUST THEM

RESOURCES

Finding a Church

We are emotional and relational beings. This was no mistake, as we are image-bearers of God (Genesis 1:27). In His perfect Triune being, It's only natural we need community to thrive.

Do we need a church building to be the Church? Absolutely not. It is not necessary, but it's certainly beneficial and biblical.

"And let us consider how to stir up one another to love and good works, not neglecting to meet together, as is the habit of some, but encouraging one another, and all the more as you see the day drawing near." *-Hebrews 10:24-25*

"Iron sharpens iron, and one man sharpens another." *-Proverbs 27:17*

If you have no idea where to start, visit these websites to help locate a church based on your geographical area and denomination preference:

- www.churchfinder.com
- www.localchurches.org
- **https://www.focusonthefamily.com/faith/looking-for-the-right-church/**

©Focus on the Family is a great resource for family and church resources.

What to look for in a church:

- The congregation is filled with believers as members.
- The leadership is qualified in doctrine and fellowship.
- The preaching and teaching is biblically accurate.
- The worship style fits your personal preference, and again, doctrinally sound.
- There's unity in the church congregation.
- Sanctification is one of the main goals.
- Bringing people to salvation is the main goal.

Don't be afraid to try out a church. Bring your family or a friend, exploring different ones in your surrounding geographical areas until you find the right fit.

Finding a Therapist

There are two types of therapists: Psychologists and Psychiatrists.

Psychologists are focused extensively on their client's emotional and mental suffering through the practice of talk therapy and behavioral intervention. On the other hand, *Psychiatrists* are medically trained professionals that can legally prescribe medication and monitor their patient's mental health journey through this course of treatment. Seeing a Psychologist is usually the first recommendation in the course of mental health treatment, followed by seeing a Psychiatrist if medical intervention is needed.

If you need someone to talk to who feels safe, check out one of these organizations (some have 24/7 access to licensed counselors):

- www.TalkSpace.com
- www.7Cups.com
- www.BetterHelp.com
- www.Breakthrough.com
- **https://proverbs31.org/about/counseling-support**

Have insurance? Check with your insurance provider, as they should have a list of therapists that are local to you.

Don't have insurance? No problem. Visit:

- www.OpenPathCollective.org to find a therapist in your area.

Do you have something specific you need help with? There are many therapists that specialize in particular areas of the mental health industry- such as eating disorders, anxiety, bipolar disorder, or marriage and family counseling. To search within a certain geographical area and insurance plan, visit:

- www.PsychologyToday.com/us/therapists

Their job is to help you explore what you need and discover the methods to get you onto your path of wellness. Your job is to find the right Christ-following therapist and support system for you. Do not be afraid to "test out" professionals, as you need to find the right fit for you.

Seeking help doesn't make you weak, friend. It makes you wise.

Our Hope

Does God truly love me?

Yes.

That was displayed at the Cross.

The thing is, we have a human problem.

"As it is written: none is righteous, no, not one;"

-Romans 3:10

"For all have sinned and fall short of the glory of God." *-Romans 3:23*

"For the wages of sin is death, but the free gift of God is eternal life in Christ Jesus our Lord." *-Romans 6:23*

We have hope in the love of God, expressed through Jesus Christ.

"But God shows His love for us in that while we were still sinners, Christ died for us." *-Romans 5:8*

"Because, if you confess with your mouth that **Jesus is Lord and believe** in your heart that God raised Him from the dead, **you will be saved**. For with the heart one believes and is justified, and with the mouth one confesses and is saved."*-Romans 10:9-10*

"For everyone who calls on the name of the Lord will be saved." *-Romans 10:13*

Salvation is our promise and inheritance in Heaven to be with Jesus.

"In Him we have obtained an inheritance, having been predestined according to the purpose of Him who works all things according to the counsel of His

will, so that we who were the first to hope in Christ might be to the praise of His glory. In Him you also, **when you heard the word of truth**, the gospel of your salvation, and **believed in Him, were sealed with the promised Holy Spirit, who is the guarantee of our inheritance until we acquire possession of it, to the praise of His glory**."
-Ephesians 1:11-14

"Therefore, since we have been **justified by faith**, **we have peace with God** through our Lord Jesus Christ. Through Him we have also obtained access by faith into this grace in which we stand, and we rejoice in hope of the glory of God." *-Romans 5:1-2*

Rejoice! For there is no condemnation now.

"There is therefore now no condemnation for those who are in Christ Jesus." *-Romans 8:1*

Walk in freedom knowing you are loved, chosen, justified, and blameless.

WHAT DOES IT LOOK LIKE TO GRACEFULLY NAVIGATE ANXIETY? IT'S CHOOSING TO...

01 SURRENDER OUR STRONGHOLDS FOR THE SAKE OF A PEACE-FILLED MIND

02 TRUST THE FATHER WITH THE PROCESS, EVEN WHEN IT'S HARD

03 HUMBLY EXPOSE OUR WEAKNESSES IN EXCHANGE FOR LOVING GUIDANCE

04 FAITHFULLY WALK UNDER THE INSTRUCTION OF THE FATHER

05 ALIGN OUR STEPS WITH HIS STEPS AS HE MINISTERS TO OUR MINDS

06 SEE OURSELVES AS HE SEES US, FIGHTING FOR THAT TRUTH

07 SEE HIS MARKINGS OF JOY IN EVERY SEASON, NO MATTER HOW SMALL THEY APPEAR

08 SEE OUR TOUGHEST STORM AND USE IT AS OUR GREATEST STRENGTH

References

Letter from the Author

1. “Pervasive Negative Beliefs – Who Made You Feel Worthless and Why Do You Believe Them?” *Huddle.care*, www.huddle.care/pervasive-negative-beliefs-who-made-you-feel-worthless-and-why-do-you-believe-them/.

“Chapter 3: The Radical Antidote: Emotional Health and Contemplative Spirituality.” *Emotionally Healthy Spirituality: It's Impossible to Be Spiritually Mature, While Remaining Emotionally Immature*, by Peter Scazzero, Zondervan, 2017, pp. 39–53.

2. *“Anxiety Disorders and Depression Research & Treatment.” Anxiety and Depression Association of America, ADAA, adaa.org/.*

3. *“Number of People Reporting Anxiety and Depression Nationwide since Start of Pandemic Hits All-Time High in September, Hitting Young People Hardest.” Mental Health America, 20 Oct. 2020, www.mhanational.org/number-people-reporting-*

anxiety-and-depression-nationwide-start-pandemic-hits-all-time-high.

4. "Anxiety Disorders and Depression Research & Treatment." Anxiety and Depression Association of America, ADAA, adaa.org/.

Introduction

1-2. Prasanna, Daniel. "The Different Ranks of Seafarers." *ToughNickel*, ToughNickel, 21 Apr. 2011, toughnickel.com/industries/ranksofseafarersresponsibilities.

Chapter 1

1. "Anxiety Disorders and Depression Research & Treatment." *Anxiety and Depression Association of America, ADAA*, adaa.org/.

2. Holland, Kimberly. "Anxiety: Causes, Symptoms, Treatment, and More." *Healthline*, Healthline Media, 3 Sept. 2020, www.healthline.com/health/anxiety.

3. "Anxiety Disorders and Depression Research & Treatment." *Anxiety and Depression Association of America, ADAA*, adaa.org/.

4. “Anxiety Disorders and Depression Research & Treatment.” *Anxiety and Depression Association of America, ADAA*, adaa.org/.

Page 36. Zung, William W.K. “A Rating Instrument For Anxiety Disorders.” *Psychosomatics*, vol. 12, no. 6, 1971, pp. 371–379., doi:10.1016/s0033-3182(71)71479-0.

Chapter 2

1. Fletcher, Jenna. “4-7-8 Breathing: How It Works, Benefits, and Uses.” *Medical News Today*, MediLexicon International, 2019, www.medicalnewstoday.com/articles/324417.

Chapter 3

1. “Anxiety Disorders and Depression Research & Treatment.” *Anxiety and Depression Association of America, ADAA*, adaa.org/.

2. Cackovic, Curt. “Panic Disorder.” *StatPearls [Internet]*., U.S. National Library of Medicine, 29 Nov. 2020, www.ncbi.nlm.nih.gov/books/NBK430973/.

“Identifying & Coping with Anxiety Triggers: The Recovery Village.” Edited by Megan Hull, *The Recovery Village Drug and Alcohol Rehab*, The Recovery Village Drug and Alcohol Rehab, 24 Dec.

2020, www.therecoveryvillage.com/mental-health/anxiety/related/anxiety-triggers/.

Chapter 4

1. Cackovic, Curt. "Panic Disorder." *StatPearls [Internet].*, U.S. National Library of Medicine, 29 Nov. 2020, www.ncbi.nlm.nih.gov/books/NBK430973/.

2. Boyes, Alice. "Cognitive Behavioral Therapy (CBT) Blog. Straightforward Guide to CBT." *Dr Alice Boyes*, 8 Apr. 2018, www.aliceboyes.com/cognitive-behavior-therapy-blog-straightforward-guide-to-cbt/.

3. Holland, Kimberly. "Anxiety: Causes, Symptoms, Treatment, and More." *Healthline*, Healthline Media, 3 Sept. 2020, www.healthline.com/health/anxiety.

4. Fletcher, Jenna. "4-7-8 Breathing: How It Works, Benefits, and Uses." *Medical News Today*, MediLexicon International, 2019, www.medicalnewstoday.com/articles/324417.

5-8. This Is Your Brain on Food: an Indispensable Guide to the Surprising Foods That Fight Depression, Anxiety, PTSD, OCD, ADHD, and More, by Uma Naidoo, Little, Brown Spark, 2020, pp. 57–80.

Chapter 5

1. Suni, Eric. "How Much Sleep Do We Really Need?" *Sleep Foundation*, 10 Mar. 2021, www.sleepfoundation.org/how-sleep-works/how-much-sleep-do-we-really-need.

2. Cackovic, Curt. "Panic Disorder." *StatPearls [Internet].*, U.S. National Library of Medicine, 29 Nov. 2020, www.ncbi.nlm.nih.gov/books/NBK430973/.

3. This Is Your Brain on Food: an Indispensable Guide to the Surprising Foods That Fight Depression, Anxiety, PTSD, OCD, ADHD, and More, by Uma Naidoo, Little, Brown Spark, 2020, pp. 57–80.

4. Kowalski HBSc, ND , Ashley. "Stress." *NPC*, 2016, www.naturopathiccurrents.com/articles/stress.

5. "Identifying & Coping with Anxiety Triggers: The Recovery Village." Edited by Megan Hull, *The Recovery Village Drug and Alcohol Rehab*, The Recovery Village Drug and Alcohol Rehab, 24 Dec. 2020, www.therecoveryvillage.com/mental-health/anxiety/related/anxiety-triggers/.

6. Hirsch, Colette R., and Andrew Mathews. "A Cognitive Model of Pathological Worry." *Behaviour Research and Therapy*, vol. 50, no. 10, 2012, pp. 636–646., doi:10.1016/j.brat.2012.06.007.

Chapter 6

1. "Chapter 3: The Radical Antidote: Emotional Health and Contemplative Spirituality." Emotionally Healthy Spirituality: It's Impossible to Be Spiritually Mature, While Remaining Emotionally Immature, by Peter Scazzero, Zondervan, 2017, pp. 39–53.

2-3. Whalley, Matthew. "Cognitive Distortions: Unhelpful Thinking Habits." *Psychology Tools*, 11 Nov. 2020, www.psychologytools.com/articles/unhelpful-thinking-styles-cognitive-distortions-in-cbt/

4-5. Keng, Shian-Ling, et al. "Effects of Mindfulness on Psychological Health: A Review of Empirical Studies." *Clinical Psychology Review*, vol. 31, no. 6, 2011, pp. 1041–1056., doi:10.1016/j.cpr.2011.04.006.

Resources

Page 180. Anxiety Charts. Katharina Star, PhD. "How to Use a Panic Attack Diary." *Verywell Mind*, 23 Jan. 2021, www.verywellmind.com/anxiety-and-panic-attack-diary-2584057.

Acknowledgments

First and foremost, my Savior, my Redeemer: There are not enough words to express my gratitude over this project. When I say, “I never saw it coming”, I truly never saw this book as a part of my story. Your lovingkindness, grace, and goodness exceed anything in this world, and I am thankful for Your Direction. You are such a good Father that shows me time and time again You only want what is best for me. I am living proof that whatever stronghold may grip hard on my life, You are mightier and faithful to walk it out with me. All of this is for Your Glory.

To my husband, Joshua: Thank you for being my constant supporter in every season we face together. Your wisdom, strength, compassion, and humor is inspiring and motivating. You push me to be the best that I can be for us and our children. Thank you for allowing space for me to be obedient in this project. I love you.

To my children, Hudson and Emerson: You two are the definition of grace and joy in my life. If I ever needed an ounce of patience, God so graciously presented it in two tiny little packages such as yourselves. You may not know it now, but you will be world-changers some day. I just have to survive raising you first.

To my parents: I owe every bit of my affectionate being to you both. You have shown so much grace, love, and loyalty to us through your marriage and personality. I am forever grateful to our Heavenly Father for matching us up through adoption. I thank you for helping Josh and I navigate through parenthood, being a literal shoulder to cry on, and rescuing us at our every call.

To my in-loves and the extended family I am happy to call mine: Bill- thank you for being such a heavenly light directing your home. Kathy- thank you for raising the epitome of a gentleman that I get the joy of calling my husband. Nicki- your sweet and giving heart is inspiring, and always pushes me out of my bubble to enjoy the simple things. The rest of my Franks, married into or by blood- I love you all dearly. You make my life happy!

To my family: I couldn't have picked a better family to grow up in, shaping me into the person I am today. I am thankful for the chaotic, yet lovingly full holiday gatherings. The selflessness and love shared among all of you is something I am proud to share with my children because of you. Phillip- I am so very thankful you are my brother. Although we didn't feel that way growing up, I love where we are now. I am proud to call you my family, and love that my children get to call you Uncle.

To my editors Michelle and Kimberly: Michelle- without your insight, wisdom, guidance, and knack for challenging me, this project might not have seen the light of day. You took this pile of mess I gave you and led me down a path of beautiful refinement, aiding in the birthing process of what we see today. You are a gem. My friend. I appreciate you more than you know! Kimberly- I thank God for adding you as another special addition to this project. You have such a grace about you and so much wisdom in guiding writers in their projects. Though our time was short together in the final stages of this book, they were not wasted and greatly added to what we see today. Thank you!

To my church family: It is an honor to live in "community" with you. The leadership of this church, both pastoral and volunteer, are inspiring and the epitome of "the hands and feet of Jesus". Keep doing the hard and holy work, DC3!

To my tribe of girlfriends: I am blessed to call so many of you my people. You each have your own special trait I absolutely adore. The leadership, selflessness, humility, wisdom, joy, and love are just some of the traits I hope to portray in my life. Natalia, thank you for your wisdom and guidance in not only this journey called "motherhood", but this book project. Thank you for your time and keeping me in check with sound doctrine and transparency. I'm grateful for you! Deby, Gaby, Erin, Lisa— thank you for cheering me on in the background with your love and support. My ladies that walk this new homeschool path with me (Michelle, Tricia, Courtney, Marla), I don't know what I would do without your support, guidance, and humility as we lead our homes together. For the unnamed that are close with me in this season of life, you guide me in motherhood and womanhood so elegantly and full of grace. My tribe, my people, I thank you.

To James Fry and Mitzi Brown: Thank you both for your leadership and guidance on this topic. Your wisdom, grace, and willingness to support this book do not go unnoticed. I appreciate both of your integration of Christian Theology with Psychology in Counseling! Mitzi- It's an honor to come together for projects such as this one. I look forward to many more in the future!

To my Beta Readers: Eddie, Christa, Eva, Michelle, Natalia, James, Mitzi, and Squeeze— your time and effort to read and help critique the manuscript makes my heart filled with gratitude and completely soar. Thank you for your willingness to refine this project and support my mess. You are so, so valued!

STAY CONNECTED

HI, THERE!

I'D LOVE TO CONNECT

I provide monthly emails with encouraging content, all with YOU in mind! You can find me on Social Media and Subscribe through the website:

www.theheatherfrank.com

@theheatherfrank

ABOUT THE AUTHOR

Heather Frank is the wife of a small-town entrepreneur and mother of two. She is an advocate for Mental Health Awareness and spreading the Gospel. She serves at her local church, is a published photographer, and holds a degree in Psychology.

As a newly homeschooling mama, Heather understands firsthand what it feels like to spiral out of control from destructive thinking. As she shares her life experiences, Heather writes with vulnerability and authenticity to encourage women to seek Jesus in any season of their lives. Her heart is to show humble transparency and the goodness of God's grace and lovingkindness in our lives.

MY NOTES

WHAT'S *stressing* ME OUT?

THE TO-DO LISTS BETWEEN MY HOME AND AT WORK ARE PILING UP. I FEEL UNSEEN BY MY HUSBAND AND UNAPPRECIATED IN THE WORK I *CAN* MANAGE TO GET DONE...

GOD, I GIVE THESE STRESSORS OVER TO YOU.

MY NOTES

MY NOTES

WHAT'S OUT OF MY *control?*

WHAT HAPPENS TO MY TEENAGE CHILDREN WHEN THEY WALK OUT MY FRONT DOOR IS OUT OF MY CONTROL. LORD, I RELEASE THE WORRY OF WHAT COULD HAPPEN INTO YOUR HANDS...

GOD, THANK YOU FOR YOUR SOVEREIGNTY.

MY NOTES

MY NOTES

WORDS OF
encouragement

JUST AS THE SCRIPTURE HAS STATED, I AM SEEN AND FIERCELY LOVED. HIS PLANS FOR ME ARE GREATER THAN I CAN IMAGINE...

GOD, THANK YOU
FOR YOUR
LOVINGKINDNESS FOUND
IN SCRIPTURE

MY NOTES

MONTH/YEAR:

	DAY	1	2	3	4	5	6	7	8	9	10
Wk 1	Sunday										
	Monday										
	Tuesday										
	Wednesday										
	Thursday										
	Friday										
	Saturday										
Wk 2	Sunday										
	Monday										
	Tuesday										
	Wednesday										
	Thursday										
	Friday										
	Saturday										
Wk 3	Sunday										
	Monday										
	Tuesday										
	Wednesday										
	Thursday										
	Friday										
	Saturday										
Wk 4	Sunday										
	Monday										
	Tuesday										
	Wednesday										
	Thursday										
	Friday										
	Saturday										

LEVEL OF ANXIETY

NOTES

"ANXIETY IN A MAN'S HEART
WEIGHS HIM DOWN,
BUT A GOOD WORD MAKES HIM GLAD."
-PROVERBS 12:25

MONTH/YEAR:

LEVEL OF ANXIETY

	DAY	1	2	3	4	5	6	7	8	9	10
Wk 1	Sunday										
	Monday										
	Tuesday										
	Wednesday										
	Thursday										
	Friday										
	Saturday										
Wk 2	Sunday										
	Monday										
	Tuesday										
	Wednesday										
	Thursday										
	Friday										
	Saturday										
Wk 3	Sunday										
	Monday										
	Tuesday										
	Wednesday										
	Thursday										
	Friday										
	Saturday										
Wk 4	Sunday										
	Monday										
	Tuesday										
	Wednesday										
	Thursday										
	Friday										
	Saturday										

NOTES

"ANXIETY IN A MAN'S HEART
WEIGHS HIM DOWN,
BUT A GOOD WORD MAKES HIM GLAD."
-PROVERBS 12:25

MONTH/YEAR:

LEVEL OF ANXIETY

	DAY	1	2	3	4	5	6	7	8	9	10
	Sunday										
	Monday										
	Tuesday										
Wk 1	Wednesday										
	Thursday										
	Friday										
	Saturday										
	Sunday										
	Monday										
	Tuesday										
Wk 2	Wednesday										
	Thursday										
	Friday										
	Saturday										
	Sunday										
	Monday										
	Tuesday										
Wk 3	Wednesday										
	Thursday										
	Friday										
	Saturday										
	Sunday										
	Monday										
	Tuesday										
Wk 4	Wednesday										
	Thursday										
	Friday										
	Saturday										

NOTES

"ANXIETY IN A MAN'S HEART
WEIGHS HIM DOWN,
BUT A GOOD WORD MAKES HIM GLAD."
-PROVERBS 12:25

MONTH/YEAR:

		LEVEL OF ANXIETY									
	DAY	1	2	3	4	5	6	7	8	9	10
	Sunday										
	Monday										
	Tuesday										
Wk 1	Wednesday										
	Thursday										
	Friday										
	Saturday										
	Sunday										
	Monday										
	Tuesday										
Wk 2	Wednesday										
	Thursday										
	Friday										
	Saturday										
	Sunday										
	Monday										
	Tuesday										
Wk 3	Wednesday										
	Thursday										
	Friday										
	Saturday										
	Sunday										
	Monday										
	Tuesday										
Wk 4	Wednesday										
	Thursday										
	Friday										
	Saturday										

NOTES

"ANXIETY IN A MAN'S HEART
WEIGHS HIM DOWN,
BUT A GOOD WORD MAKES HIM GLAD."
-PROVERBS 12:25

MONTH/YEAR:

LEVEL OF ANXIETY

	DAY	1	2	3	4	5	6	7	8	9	10
Wk 1	Sunday										
	Monday										
	Tuesday										
	Wednesday										
	Thursday										
	Friday										
	Saturday										
Wk 2	Sunday										
	Monday										
	Tuesday										
	Wednesday										
	Thursday										
	Friday										
	Saturday										
Wk 3	Sunday										
	Monday										
	Tuesday										
	Wednesday										
	Thursday										
	Friday										
	Saturday										
Wk 4	Sunday										
	Monday										
	Tuesday										
	Wednesday										
	Thursday										
	Friday										
	Saturday										

NOTES

"ANXIETY IN A MAN'S HEART
WEIGHS HIM DOWN,
BUT A GOOD WORD MAKES HIM GLAD."
-PROVERBS 12:25

MONTH/YEAR:

LEVEL OF ANXIETY

	DAY	1	2	3	4	5	6	7	8	9	10
	Sunday										
	Monday										
	Tuesday										
Wk 1	Wednesday										
	Thursday										
	Friday										
	Saturday										
	Sunday										
	Monday										
	Tuesday										
Wk 2	Wednesday										
	Thursday										
	Friday										
	Saturday										
	Sunday										
	Monday										
	Tuesday										
Wk 3	Wednesday										
	Thursday										
	Friday										
	Saturday										
	Sunday										
	Monday										
	Tuesday										
Wk 4	Wednesday										
	Thursday										
	Friday										
	Saturday										

NOTES

"ANXIETY IN A MAN'S HEART
WEIGHS HIM DOWN,
BUT A GOOD WORD MAKES HIM GLAD."
-PROVERBS 12:25

ANXIETY TRACKER

MY NOTES

MY NOTES

MY NOTES

MY NOTES

"But now thus says the Lord,
He who created you, O Jacob,
He who formed you, O Israel:
"**Fear not, for I have redeemed you;
I have called you by name, you are mine.**"

-Isaiah 43:1

CPSIA information can be obtained
at www.ICGtesting.com
Printed in the USA
LVHW080147260721
693670LV00002B/30

9 781737 453307